ENGLISH FOR WORK

EVERYDAY
TECHNICAL
ENGLISH

Valerie Lambert and Elaine Murray

Longman

Pearson Education Limited
Edinburgh Gate, Harlow,
Essex, CM20 2JE, England
and Associated Companies throughout the world

www.longman.com

First published 2003
Seventh impression 2009

ISBN 978-0-582-53963-1

Set in Univers Condensed 10pt
Printed in China   SWTC/07

Designed and typeset by Rock Graphics

Illustrations by Roger Fereday

This book is dedicated to the memory of Graham Lambert
– a man of great courage and determination.

Acknowledgements
We would especially like to thank Ian Badger, Teresa Miller and Eileen Wasserman for their valuable comments and assistance throughout the writing process and the many students from UPM-Kymmene, Metso Paper, Goldwell GmbH and BMES for their help in piloting the materials.

Cover photograph copyright © Getty Images – Stuart Hunter

Contents

Introduction

English for Work

The books in this series present and practise spoken English and practical writing for everyday communication; they feature key words and expressions which will help you in a wide range of work situations. The target language is introduced through short dialogues and texts, and developed in language notes and practice exercises.

The dialogues are recorded on an accompanying CD. The accents featured are predominantly British English, but comments on American usage are included in the notes.

At the back of each book there is a glossary which contains highlighted language from the dialogues. Translations of the glossary can be downloaded, in selected languages, from the Longman website, **www.longman-elt.com**.

The series is intended for pre-intermediate/intermediate level learners.

Everyday Technical English

Everyday Technical English is suitable for people already working in an industrial or technical environment, and for students in adult education classes, schools, colleges and universities.

The book concentrates on the core everyday technical language used across a variety of industries. We have tried to keep to a minimum the use of language related to specific industries. A small amount of simple industry-specific language is sometimes used, however, to give a context to a dialogue.

In order to widen your knowledge of the language you might need in your work, you may find it useful to refer to the other titles in the *English for Work* series:

Everyday Business English
Business Presentations
Everyday Business Writing

How to use the book

You can work through the book from start to finish or choose a unit depending on your work needs.

Start a unit by listening to and repeating the *Useful phrases*. Then listen to the dialogues and study the accompanying notes. Certain phrases have been highlighted that have particular language features associated with them. However, it is worthwhile noting other phrases that appear in the dialogues, which are equally important and can also be seen as key phrases. There is a word list at the back of the book which gives simple explanations in English of less familiar vocabulary items. You can also use a dictionary if necessary to check your understanding of the language presented.

On the notes pages you will find boxes containing notes on the key differences between everyday British and American usage.

After studying the dialogues and notes, work through the exercises. You can refer back to the dialogues and notes as necessary and also use a dictionary to check any new language. Answers are given at the end of the book.

Finally, refer to the glossary at the back of the book and test yourself on your understanding of key expressions. Write translations of these expressions, again using a dictionary if necessary. Visit the *English for Work* page on the Longman website, www.longman-elt.com where you will find translations of the key phrases in a number of languages.

You can use this book for self study or with a teacher. Good luck and enjoy building your 'Everyday Technical English' skills!

Valerie Lambert and Elaine Murray, 2003

Some recommended materials to accompany the *English for Work* series:
Longman Business English Dictionary
Penguin Quick Guides: Business English Phrases
Penguin Quick Guides: Business English Verbs
Penguin Quick Guides: Business English Words
Penguin Quick Guides: Computer English

1 Working in industry

Some useful phrases.
Listen to the recording and repeat.

I work for a large, multinational company.
We manufacture components for our car production plants in Europe.
The company has operations in over fifty countries.
We export to Eastern Europe and the Far East.
The domestic market accounts for about 40 per cent of our total production.

The company was founded in 1960.
We have over sixty employees.
What's your annual turnover?
What does IABS stand for?

What does your job involve?
I'm in charge of twenty-five assembly workers.
I have to liaise with our inspectors.
Who do you report to?

I'm on flexi-time.
Do you do overtime?
We have a three-shift system.
I'm on the early shift.

7

Dialogues 1

A manufacturing company

A: So, who do you work for?

B: I work for a large multinational company called DAK Group. We have five main areas of business – construction, heavy industry, shipbuilding, motor vehicles and telecommunications.

A: And which side of the business do you work in?

B: The motor vehicles division. I work in our Belgian factory. We manufacture components for our car production plants in Europe.

A: Where are DAK headquarters?

B: In Seoul. But the company has operations in over fifty countries and thirty factories all over the world.

Products and markets

A: What does your company do exactly?

B: We design and assemble a wide range of electric generators for hospitals, hotels and small factories. We specialise in medium-sized generators but we're hoping to diversify into larger models next year.

A: And who do you sell to?

B: We export to Eastern Europe and the Far East. The domestic market accounts for about 40 per cent of our total sales.

Company size

A: How many people does your company employ?

B: We have over sixty employees. We have about forty factory workers and technical people and the rest are admin and sales staff. We started off with only ten people so our workforce has grown a lot.

A: What's your annual turnover?

B: It was just over two million euros last year.

Company background

A: How long has the company been in business?

B: For over forty years. The original company – Davies Engineering – was founded in 1960 by the Davies brothers in a small workshop near Manchester. They closed down the workshop in 1980 and opened up a new factory in Leeds.

A: When did it become IABS?

B: In 1997 – when it was bought by a German company. They set up two more businesses in the UK.

A: What does IABS stand for?

B: International Air Braking Systems.

Notes

I work for a large multinational company …
Other ways of talking about company size:
It's a medium-sized firm.
It's a small, family-owned business.

We manufacture components …
Note the use of the present simple for situations which are generally true (**NOT** *We are manufacturing …*):
We produce parts for the shipbuilding industry.
We make boxes for packaging firms.

… for our car production plants in Europe.
Note the use of *for*.
A *plant* is a place where things are produced:
a power plant, a steel plant.

… the company has operations in over fifty countries …
Other ways of talking about parts of the company in other countries:
We have factories all over Europe.
We have production/warehousing facilities in more than twenty countries.

We specialise in medium-sized generators …
Note the use of *specialise in* to refer to the main products of a company.

We export to Eastern Europe and the Far East.
Note: *the UK, the US, the EU, the Middle East.*
No *the* with most countries or continents:
France, Australia, South America.

The domestic market accounts for about 40 per cent of our total sales.
Note the use of *account(s) for*:
Exports account for 60 per cent of our total production.
Hotel generators account for about 10 per cent of our range of products.

We have over sixty employees.
Other ways of talking about the number of employees:
We employ 2 000 people in our Lyons factory.
There are 200 people working here.

We have about forty factory workers and technical people …
Note the use of *people*: *our maintenance people, our production people.*

… the rest are admin and sales staff.
Admin is short for *administrative.*

… our workforce has grown a lot.
Workforce is often used for people who work for an industrial company:
We need to reduce our workforce.

What's your annual turnover?
Annual turnover is the money that comes into the business each year (through sales, services, etc.).

The original company was founded in 1960 …
was founded means *was started.* Note the use of the passive. Other examples of passive usage:
It was bought by a German company.
It was taken over last year.

What does IABS stand for?
We use *stand for* when we want to know what letters in a name represent:
BP stands for British Petroleum.

British/American differences	
British	**American**
Which side of the business do you work in?	*Which part of the business do you work in?* (also used in British English)
… for our car production plants	*… for our auto(mobile) production plants*
specialise	*specialize*

Dialogues 2

Training

A: What do you do?

B: I'm an apprentice with a local engineering firm. My training lasts for two years. Two days a week I study Engineering at a local college. If I pass all my exams, I hope the company will take me on as an engineer.

Job responsibilities

A: What does your job involve?

B: I'm the Project Manager so I have to make sure our projects run smoothly. I work with three Project Engineers. They take care of after-sales service and look after the maintenance side of the business.

Being in charge

A: I'm a foreman in our assembly shop. I'm in charge of about twenty-five assembly workers. I have to liaise very closely with our inspectors. It's their job to check the quality of the work.

B: Who do you report to?

A: I report to the Shift Supervisor, and he reports to the Factory Manager.

Team-working

A: Tell me about how you work here.

B: We work in teams. There are about four to six people in each team. I'm training to be a team leader. Each team member is responsible for the quality of the goods we produce. We are multi-skilled so we can rotate jobs. I like that. It stops the work getting boring.

Hours and holidays

A: How many hours do you work a week?

B: I do a forty-hour week. I'm on flexi-time. I usually start work at 8 a.m. and finish at 4:30 and have half an hour for lunch. But I can start and finish earlier or later if I want.

A: And how many weeks holiday do you get a year?

B: Four – plus public holidays. I usually take two weeks off in the summer and the rest at New Year.

A: Do you do overtime?

B: Yes, if we're busy. I'm paid double-time if I work at weekends.

Shift systems

A: What sort of shift-system do you operate?

B: We have a three-shift system – that's three eight-hour shifts each weekday. We're shut at weekends. This week I'm on the early shift.

A: Do you ever have to do the night shift?

B: Yes, sometimes. I don't like working nights – I have problems sleeping during the day.

Notes

I'm an apprentice ...
> You can also say:
> *I'm a trainee.*
> *I'm doing an apprenticeship.*

... I hope the company will take me on as an engineer.
> To *take on* someone means to employ someone.

What does your job involve?
> This is how we ask about job duties. If *involve* is followed by a verb, use *–ing*:
> *My job involves checking the safety of our equipment.*

... I have to make sure our projects run smoothly.
> Some other ways of talking about job responsibilities and duties:
> *I take care of after-sales service.*
> *I look after the maintenance side of the business.*
> *It's my job to check quality.*

I'm in charge of about twenty-five assembly workers.
> This means you are the person in control and you have responsibility. Note: **NOT** *I am the responsible of the workshop.*

I have to liaise very closely with our inspectors.
> To *liaise* means to work closely with someone.

Who do you report to?
> This is how we ask who someone's immediate boss is.

Each team member is responsible for the quality of the goods we produce.
> Note the use of *for* after *responsible*. A verb must be in the *–ing* form:
> *He's responsible for ordering spare parts.*

We are multi-skilled so we can rotate jobs.
> This means you are skilled in many areas. To *rotate jobs* means to take it in turns to do different jobs.

I'm on flexi-time.
> This means your hours are flexible. You don't work fixed hours.

I usually take two weeks off in the summer ...
> Note the use of *off* to mean *not working*.
> *She's off sick today.*
> *I'm having New Year's Day off this year.*

Do you do overtime?
> This means to work extra time, in addition to your normal hours.
> *I'm working overtime this weekend.*

I'm paid double-time if I work at weekends.
> This means you will earn twice what you normally earn.

We have a three-shift system ...
> Note: **NOT** *a three-shifts system.*
> Note the use of *hour*, **NOT** *hours*:
> *Three eight-hour shifts.*
> *A 40-hour week.*

... I'm on the early shift.
> Note the use of *on*. Other ways of talking about shifts:
> *I'm doing the night shift this week.*
> *I don't like working nights.*

British/American differences

British	American
to take someone on	to hire someone
(Both British and American English also use the phrase *to employ someone*.)	
in each team	on each team
flexi-time	flextime
holiday	vacation
I'm paid double-time if I work at weekends.	I'm paid double-time if I work on weekends.
We're closed/shut at weekends.	We're closed/shut on the weekend.
top-of-the-range cars, p12	top-of-the-line cars
mobile phone, p13	cell(ular) phone
the automotive industry, p13	the auto(mobile) industry
fitter, p14	carpenter would be used here (also used in British English to refer only to people who work with wood)

Practice

1 Write down a question from the dialogues for the following responses.

EXAMPLE: Who do you sell to? ....
We sell mainly to domestic packaging companies.

a ....?
An electronics company called Eurotron.

b ....?
We design jet engines.

c ....?
We have over 1 000 employees worldwide.

d ....?
I'm a computer engineer.

e ....?
My job involves liaising carefully with our production people to plan our
production schedules.

f ....?
I report to our shift supervisor.

g ....?
I work on average thirty-five hours a week.

h ....?
Just over two million dollars a year.

2 Complete the sentences with a preposition.

EXAMPLE: I'm .... on .... the afternoon shift this week.

a We produce components .... the car industry.

b Exports account .... 70 per cent of total sales.

c We have factories all .... the world.

d We specialise .... top-of-the-range cars.

e We're trying to diversify .... more expensive models.

f What does IBM stand ....?

g He's responsible .... Quality Control.

h I'm in charge .... the workshop.

i Who takes care .... after-sales service?

j I have to liaise .... our production planners.

3 Complete the sentences using a word from the box below.

apprentice	components	flexi-time	workforce	shift
~~turnover~~	operations	plant	people	overtime

EXAMPLE: Our .. turnover .... this year will be about $500 000.

a   I'm doing . . . . this week so I'll earn more money.

b   My son is an . . . . at a local furniture factory.

c   She works . . . . so she can start work any time between
    8 a.m. and 9 a.m.

d   Our company has . . . . in more than twenty countries.

e   What . . . . are you on this week?

f   Our . . . . has been cut because we don't have enough orders.

g   They manufacture electronic . . . . for computers.

h   Our maintenance . . . . do all our repairs.

i   DAK is opening a new car . . . . in the UK next year.

4 Match the products and industries. Use a dictionary to help you if necessary.

1	diesel oil	a	the pharmaceutical industry.
2	car components	b	the construction industry.
3	buildings	c	the textile industry.
4	drugs	d	the electronics industry.
5	jet engines	e	the petrochemical industry.
6	cardboard boxes	f	the aerospace industry.
7	semi-conductors	g	the telecommunications industry.
8	gold	h	the automotive industry.
9	cloth	i	the packaging industry.
10	mobile phones	j	the mining industry.

5 Add a verb to the preposition to make a two-part verb.

EXAMPLE: The company is planning to . . . . . open . . . . up a factory in China next year.

a   We will have to . . . . **on** some more machine operators as we are
    behind with orders.

b   Our IT people . . . . **after** the maintenance of our computer systems.

c   They had to . . . . **down** their German factory because costs were too high.

d   I'm going to . . . . **off** the whole of July this year. I need a good holiday.

e   I would like to become self-employed and . . . . **up** my own car
    repair business.

6 Add *the* if necessary to these geographical areas.

EXAMPLE: *The* . . . . Far East

a   . . . . European Union (EU)

b   . . . . South-East Asia

c   . . . . China

d   . . . . South America

e   . . . . United States (US)

f   . . . . United Kingdom (UK)

g   . . . . Russia

h   . . . . Western Europe

i   . . . . Germany

j   . . . . Middle East

7 Match the following descriptions with one of the jobs below. Use your dictionary if necessary.

| production planner   electronic engineer   ~~joiner~~   mechanic   fitter |
| machine operator   inspector   welder   electrician   lab technician |

EXAMPLE: Someone who works with wood: . *joiner* . . . .

a   Someone who works in a laboratory: . . . .

b   Someone who works with a machine on a production line: . . . .

c   Someone who puts together, adjusts or installs machinery or equipment: . . . .

d   Someone who works with electrical equipment: . . . .

e   Someone who joins metal together, usually using heat: . . . .

f   Someone who repairs and maintains engines, especially car engines: . . . .

g   Someone who checks the quality of work or goods: . . . .

h   Someone who schedules the order of production runs: . . . .

i   Someone who works with things like computers, TVs, radios, etc.: . . . .

② A tour of the workplace

Some useful phrases.
Listen to the recording and repeat.

We used to be on an industrial estate.
We moved to a greenfield site last year.
I'd like to show you the layout of the factory.
This is the main factory area.

What's going on over there?
The goods are being wrapped and loaded onto pallets.
They're setting up the machine for a new run.
How long does that usually take?

Would you like me to show you our new cleaning unit?
This is our newest machine.
What's the running speed of the machine?
Our maximum output is 160 000 tonnes per annum.

It passes through a series of rollers.
Most of the water is extracted.
Is the factory fully-automated?
Some of the work is still done manually.

IS THE FACTORY FULLY AUTOMATED?

Dialogues 1

Arriving

Ⓐ: I'm phoning about the factory visit next Friday. What should I do when I arrive?

Ⓑ: **Park in the visitors' car park in front of the factory** and then go to the gatehouse. It's directly opposite the entrance to the car park. The Security people will sign you in and give you a visitor's badge. My assistant will come down to meet you.

Ⓐ: OK, thanks. Look forward to seeing you on Friday, then.

Location

Ⓐ: Have you always been on this site?

Ⓑ: No, **we used to be on an industrial estate on the outskirts of York.**

Ⓐ: Why did you move?

Ⓑ: **We needed larger premises** so **we moved to this greenfield site last year.** It's nearer the motorway so it's better for transportation.

Describing the layout

Good morning, everybody. Welcome to IAM Technology. I'm very pleased so many of you could make it here today. My name's Sam Weiss. I'm the Production Manager. **I'd like to show you the layout of the factory** before we go and visit it. As you can see from this diagram, everything is under one roof. We've designed it this way to help the flow of materials and to avoid bottlenecks.

This area here is where we keep our raw materials. **The main production area – our machine hall – is situated next to it.** Maintenance is situated between the stores and the production area. Just to the right of Maintenance, there are steps up to the Lab and the Admin Section. Process Control is also on the upper level. It's located above the factory floor so that the operators can monitor everything that is going on below.

Showing a visitor around

Ⓐ: OK, so **this is the main factory area**. We're now walking past the printing machine. It's printing in four colours at the moment.

Ⓑ: **What's going on over there?**

Ⓐ: **They're setting up the machine for a new run.**

Ⓑ: **How long does that usually take?**

Ⓐ: About twenty minutes.

Ⓑ: What's happening at the far end?

Ⓐ: That's the packing line. **The goods are being wrapped and loaded onto pallets** ready for transportation.

Notes

Park in the visitors' car park in front of the factory ...

Some other expressions to describe location:
It's directly opposite the entrance to the car park.
The power plant is on the left.
The staff canteen is behind the main warehouse.

... we used to be on an industrial estate on the outskirts of York.

Outskirts means the edge of a town/area.
Note *used to* is used when the past situation is no longer true.
We used to have a sales office but it closed down last year.

We needed larger premises ...

Premises means the buildings and land occupied by a business. Note *premises* is always plural.

... we moved to this greenfield site last year.

A *greenfield* site is a completely new site. A *brownfield* site is a redeveloped area.

I'd like to show you the layout of the factory ...

Other ways of starting a talk:
I'd like to explain our production process.
I'll say a few words about our products.
I'll tell you a bit about our company first.

The main production area – our machine hall – is situated next to it.

Some more ways of talking about where things are:
Maintenance is situated between the stores and the production area.
It's just to the right of Maintenance.

... this is the main factory area.

Note the use of *this* to show something that is near. *That* is used for something which is not so near.
This is the machine shop.
What's that over there?

What's going on over there?

Note we use the present continuous for something happening at the time of speaking:
We're now going into our finished goods area.

They're setting up the machine for a new run.

To *set up* means to prepare. A *run* means the production of the same goods during a period of time:
We'll do a trial run of 10 000.
The longer the production run, the lower the unit cost.

How long does that usually take?

How to ask about the time needed for a job. Note the present simple:
How long does it take to load up the trucks?
It takes twenty minutes to set up the machine.

The goods are being wrapped and loaded onto pallets ...

Goods are things that are produced to be sold. It is a plural noun. Note the passive (*is/are being done*) for what is happening now:
The boiler is being repaired at the moment.
The settings are being changed.

British/American differences

British	American
car park	parking lot
the gatehouse	the security building/ the guardhouse
Look forward to seeing you on Friday, then.	
(American English does not usually use *then* at the end of a sentence.)	
be on an industrial estate	be in an industrial park
this greenfield site	similar to *this undeveloped site*
a brownfield site	similar to *a redeveloped site*
(The terms *brownfield* and *greenfield* are not used in American English.)	
motorway	freeway/expressway/ Interstate
the stores	the supplies
colour	color

Dialogues 2

A new installation

A: **Would you like me to show you our new cleaning unit?** It's a clever design.

B: Yes, I'd like to see that. What does it clean exactly?

A: It washes the solvent off all the metal parts – the blades, trays etc. – and then sends it back into the system.

B: **What does the unit consist of?**

A: Well, it's basically two tanks – one for the dirty solvent and one for the clean solvent – a pump and a washing unit. Oh, and there's a cooling system and a filter. It's all controlled by a PLC system – that stands for Process Logic Control.

Speed and capacity

A: OK, so **this is our newest machine**. It was only installed last year.

B: **What's the running speed of the machine?**

A: About 1 500 metres per minute. It's one of the fastest in the world. We had a few problems with it after start-up but it's running very well now.

B: And what's the maximum output?

A: **If we're running at full capacity,** **it's 160 000 tonnes per annum.**

Explaining the process

A: Could you explain the paper-making process to us – in very simple terms – please?

B: Well, **the pulp falls from a box onto the first part of the paper machine**, which is basically a wire bed with large holes in it, where **most of the water is extracted**.

A: So, is it actually paper at this stage?

B: Yes, it is. But we need to take out more water. So **it then passes through a series of rollers,** where more water is squeezed out. After that it goes through the dryers, which are at a very high temperature. The paper is then coated. And finally it's wound onto reels and cut down into smaller lengths.

Automation

A: **Is the factory fully-automated?**

B: Not completely. Our production process is partially-automated. We use robots on the production line for routine assembly jobs but **some of the work is still done manually.**

A: What about supply of parts to the production line?

B: Well, the parts are automatically selected from the store room using **a bar-code system**. And there is an automatic feeder which takes them to the conveyor belt at the start of the production line.

A: What about the smaller components?

B: They're transported to the workstations on automated vehicles – robot trucks – which run on guide rails around the factory.

Notes

Would you like me to show you our new cleaning unit?

Note: **NOT** *Would you like that I show you...?*
Note other ways of offering/inviting:
Would you like to see the bottling plant?
Shall I show you the workshop?

What does the unit consist of?

Other ways to say this:
What are the different parts of the unit?
What's the unit made up of?

... this is our newest machine.

Note how short adjectives have *-est* added.
Long adjectives have *most* before them:
It's the latest technology.
Our most complex design is this one.
This is the most difficult part of our process.

What's the running speed of the machine?

Other ways of asking about production capability:
What's the maximum output?
What's the capacity of your plant?
How many pieces do you produce per hour?

If we're running at full capacity ...

This means if the factory is producing as much as it can.
We're only at half capacity.
It's running at three-quarters capacity at the moment.

... it's 160 000 tonnes per annum.

Note *per annum* means each year. It is less formal to say *a* for *per/each*.
It produces over 100 boxes per minute.
It uses 50KW a day.

... the pulp falls from a box onto the first part of the paper machine, ...

Note the present simple to describe processes. Also the use of *onto* and *into* to describe movement:
The plates go into an oven for drying.
The pallets are loaded onto lorries.

... most of the water is extracted.

Note the passive. This is commonly used in process description:
The paper is then coated.
The components are tested individually.

... it then passes through a series of rollers, ...

Then shows that something happens next in a process. Other commonly used markers:
First ... Next ... After that ... Finally ... .

Is the factory fully-automated?

Other useful phrases about automation:
Our production process is partially-automated.
They are transported on automated vehicles.
Automation is responsible for many job losses.

... some of the work is still done manually.

This means using people not machines. We can also say *by hand.*
Most of our workers are manual workers.
Our goods are packed manually/by hand.

... a bar-code system.

This is a label with stripes of different thickness which uniquely identify a product. It can be read by a scanner.

British/American differences

British	American
About 1 500 metres per minute.	*About one mile a minute.*

The metric system is not in general use in American English, but certain industries in the USA may use it for manufacturing.

It's 160 000 tonnes per annum.	

An American ton is 2 000 pounds (short ton). A British ton is 2 240 pounds (long ton). *Tonne* is not a British spelling of ton but a separate metric unit equal to 1 000 kg.

to run on guide rails	*to run on tracks*
lorry/lorries	*truck/trucks*

(*truck* is occasionally used in British English)

fibres, p21	*fibers*
steel works, p22	*steel mill*

Practice

1 Rewrite these sentences in the correct passive form – present simple or present continuous.

EXAMPLE: They are setting up the machine for a new run.

The machine is being set up for a new run.

a   We make the smaller models in our French factory.

....

b   We print the paper on both sides.

....

c   They are repairing the A-line at the moment.

....

d   The machine then winds the plastic onto reels.

....

e   We change the blades twice a week.

....

f   The men are loading the finished goods onto lorries.

....

g   They are building a new plant just outside Cape Town.

....

h   A machine selects the components automatically.

....

2 Complete the sentences with a preposition.

EXAMPLE: We're located .... *in* ..... an industrial zone.

a   What's going on . . . . the far end of the production line?

b   The goods are loaded . . . . pallets.

c   I look forward . . . . seeing you next week.

d   What does it consist . . . .?

e   It is cut . . . . smaller lengths.

f   We moved . . . . this site last year.

g   We're running . . . . half capacity at the moment.

h   . . . . this stage the metal is painted.

i   The fabric then passes . . . . a series of rollers.

j   Welcome . . . . HLB Engineering.

3 Complete the sentences with the words from the box.

premises	capacity	layout	gatehouse	~~level~~
	bar-codes	estate	brownfield	conveyor	outskirts

EXAMPLE: The laboratory is situated on the upper . . . . . . *level* . . . .

a   Our warehouse is located on the . . . . of the city.

b   If we build on a . . . . site, it will be much cheaper.

c   When you arrive, go to the . . . . to get a visitor's badge.

d   The . . . . belt transports goods around the factory.

e   We're moving to new . . . . next year.

f   The . . . . on every product allow us to identify them.

g   We're not running at full . . . . at present.

h   This diagram shows the . . . . of the factory.

i   We're located on an industrial . . . . by the motorway.

4 Rewrite these sentences about the paper-making process in the passive. Then put them in the right order.

EXAMPLE: a   The paper machine dries the paper with hot air.   **Order**

   The paper is dried with hot air . . . . | 7 |

b   A container drops the pulp onto the paper machine.

. . . .

c   A machine breaks down the pieces of wood into fibres.

. . . .

d   A machine mixes the fibres with water to make pulp.

. . . .

e   A machine cuts the wood into little pieces.

. . . .

f   Someone transports the reels to the customers.

. . . .

g   Someone cuts down the trees.

. . . .

h   The paper machine extracts water from the paper.

. . . .

i   The paper machine winds the paper onto reels.

. . . .

5 Match the questions and answers.

1	How long does it usually take?	a	Two tanks and a cooling system.
2	What's the maximum output?	b	No, we moved here last year.
3	What does it consist of?	c	No, only partially.
4	What's the running speed?	d	About twenty minutes.
5	Have you always been on this site?	e	1 500 metres per minute.
6	Is the factory fully-automated?	f	About 50 000 tonnes per annum.

6 Choose a word from the box to make the name of a place where something is produced or processed. Use a dictionary if necessary.

factory	mine	~~station~~	yard	refinery	works	mill	reactor

EXAMPLE: power *station* . . . .

a   oil . . . .

b   steel . . . .

c   coal . . . .

d   ship . . . .

e   nuclear . . . .

f   chocolate . . . .

g   cotton . . . .

7 Fill in the gaps with a preposition (or prepositions) to show location.

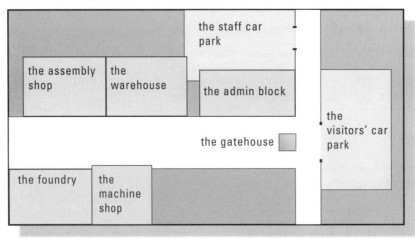

a   The warehouse is . . . . the assembly shop and the admin block.

b   The foundry is . . . . the machine shop.

c   The gatehouse is . . . . the entrance to the visitors' car park.

d   The staff car park is . . . . the admin block.

e   The warehouse is . . . . the machine shop.

f   The admin block is . . . . the warehouse.

3 Tools and equipment

Some useful phrases.
Listen to the recording and repeat.

We've got very good workshop facilities.
We do all our own servicing.
Is there anything you don't do in-house?
We send it out for maintenance.

I need something to tighten this up.
Where can I find a spare hose?
How many do you need?
We don't have any in stock.

It's a really useful piece of equipment.
What's it used for?
What does it look like?
It's made of metal.

I need to measure the length of this workbench.
We're going to replace it.
Could we increase it by about a third?
We need a piece of wood 3.5 m long by 1 m wide.

Dialogues 1

Workshop facilities

A: **We've got very good workshop facilities** here. **We do all our own servicing** and most repairs. We have separate areas for welding, grinding and sawing.

B: **Is there anything you don't do in-house?**

A: Yes. If we don't have the facilities to deal with it here, **we send it out for maintenance.**

B: Is that more expensive?

A: It depends on the job. **It's actually more cost-effective** than buying specialist equipment that we don't use very often.

The right tool for the job

A: Can you help me? This fitting has come loose and **I need something to tighten it up.**

B: Let's have a look. Oh yes, you need a 10 mm ring spanner. Here you are. Just leave it on the workbench when you finish.

A: Thanks for your help.

B: **No problem.**

In the storeroom

A: **Where can I find a spare hose** for the pump?

B: What size do you need?

A: 25 mm diameter.

B: **They're at the back of the stores, second shelf up on the right-hand side.**

A: Thanks. Have you got any light bulbs?

B: They're in the blue cupboard. Anything else?

A: Oh yes, some wire cutters.

B: I'll need to check. Sorry, **we don't have any in stock.** But I can order some and send through the order today. **How many do you need?**

A: Just one pair.

B: Fine. They should be here **the day after tomorrow.**

An unfamiliar piece of equipment

A: I haven't seen this machine before. **What's it used for?**

B: **It's a really useful piece of equipment.** It's for smoothing rough edges. Here let me show you how it works. It's very simple to operate.

Notes

We've got very good workshop facilities ...

Note the use of *facilities* for equipment.

We do all our own servicing ...

We can also say:
We handle our own servicing.
We carry out most repairs here.

Is there anything you don't do in-house?

in-house means in the company or on site.
We have our own in-house design specialists.

... we send it out for maintenance.

Note the use of *send out*, for things not done in-house.

It's actually more cost-effective ...

cost-effective means *cheaper, better value for money.*

... I need something to tighten it up.

Other examples:
I need something to seal this valve.
Have you got something I can use to make this hole bigger?
I'm looking for something to support this drum.

No problem.

Some other ways of responding:
You're welcome.
Glad to help.

Where can I find a spare hose ...?

Other ways of asking:
Where do you keep the adhesives?
Can you tell me where the bearings are stored?
I'm looking for a pair of pliers.

They're at the back of the stores, second shelf up on the right-hand side.

Note how to describe where things are:
They're on the top shelf.
You'll find them on the bottom shelf.
They're under the plastic sheet in the corner of the warehouse.

... we don't have any in stock.

Other useful expressions:
We've run out of that component.
We haven't got any of those left.

How many do you need?

Note the use of *many* with countable nouns:
How many bulbs do you want?
We don't hold many spare parts in stock.

We use *much* with uncountable nouns:
How much time do you need?
There isn't much equipment on site.

... the day after tomorrow.

Note the following expressions:
the week after next
the day before yesterday

What's it used for?

We can also say:
What do you use this for?
What does this do?

It's a really useful piece of equipment.

Note equipment is uncountable.
Note: **NOT** *equipments*.
We're going to invest in some new equipment.
machines is used in the plural as it is a countable noun.
We're going to install two new packing machines.

British/American differences	
British	**American**
We've got very good workshop facilities.	(*got* in this sense is not used in American English)
specialist equipment	*specialized equipment*
This fitting has come loose.	*This fixture has come loose.*
a 10 mm ring spanner	*a half-inch box end wrench*

Note: Wrench sets come in both metric sizes and in quarter, half, and three-quarter inch sizes.

mm, cm, m, kg
Note: The United States uses *inch* (*in.*), *foot* (*ft.*), *yard* (*yd.*), and *mile* for units of length and *ounce* (*oz.*) and *pound* (*lb.*) for units of weight.

Dialogues 2

An inventory

A: I've just taken a spanner set from the stores.

B: That's fine. **Don't forget to update the inventory!**

A: Sorry, what do you mean?

B: When you take something out of the stores you need to update the stores database so we know when to reorder.

Measurements

A: Hi Sven, **can you help me?** Could you hold the end of the tape measure, please?

B: Of course, where do you want me to stand?

A: Just there by the door. **I need to measure the length of this workbench. We're going to replace it.** OK – 3 m 47 cm. **Let's round it up to 3 m 50.**

B: I'm glad you're replacing it. We need more space to work on things. How deep will the new workbench be?

A: Tell me what size you want and I'll order the wood.

B: Well, it's about 65 cm at the moment. **Could we increase it by about a third?**

A: Sure. So let's see. **We need a piece of wood 3.5 m long by 1 m wide.** I'll order it right away and I'll be able to **install it next Tuesday.**

The wrong size

A: **Can you shorten this pipe** for me? It's too long.

B: Sure. I'll do it after lunch. What length do you need?

A: **Can you take 15 mm off it?**

B: Yes, no problem. It'll be ready by 2 p.m.

Describing things

A: Has my package arrived?

B: I'm not sure. **What does it look like?**

A: It's quite a delicate piece of equipment, so I hope it was well-packed. **It's oblong-shaped,** about 50 cm long. **It's made of metal.**

B: There's a large wooden crate in the corner which I haven't unpacked yet. It might be in there.

Notes

Don't forget to update the inventory!

We can also say:
Remember to update the inventory!
Note the following expressions:
to take an inventory
to do a stock check

... can you help me?

Note the different ways of asking someone to do something:
Could you lift this for me?
Would you mind helping me move this?
Note the use of the *-ing* form after *Would you mind ...?*

I need to measure the length of this workbench.

The adjective is *long* and the noun *length*.
Note also:
It's 50 cm wide./The width is 50cm.
It's 5 m deep./It has a depth of 5 m.
It's 1.5 m high./The height is 1.5 m.

We're going to replace it.

Note *going to* to talk about plans.
We're going to increase sales.

Lets round it up to 3 m 50.

Note the following example:
It weighs 99.5 kg, let's say 100, rounded up to the nearest full kilogram.

Could we increase it ...

We could also say:
Could you make it longer?

... by about a third?

Other useful expressions:
We need to cut it in half.
Make it twice as long.
Divide it into quarters.

We need a piece of wood 3.5 m long by 1 m wide.

Note how we give dimensions:
It's 90 cm by 60 by 50.
The shelves are 65 cm deep.
The pipe is 1 m in diameter.

... install it next Tuesday.

install means put in and make ready for use.

Can you shorten this pipe ...?

Note the verb forms:
shorten = to make shorter
widen = to make wider
lengthen = to make longer
tighten = to make tighter
loosen = to make looser

Can you take 15 mm off it?

We can also say:
Can you reduce the length by 15 mm?
I need to shorten it. (see note above)

What does it look like?

We can also say:
Can you describe it to me?

It's oblong-shaped, ...

Note the following ways of describing shapes:
It's square-shaped. It's a square.
It's shaped like a cube.
It's rectangular. It's a triangle.
It's shaped like the letter S.

It's made of metal.

Note the prepositions.
It's made of steel.
It's made by a German company.
They're made by hand.

British/American differences

British	American
spanner set	*wrench set*

(*An adjustable spanner* in British English is a *monkey wrench* in American English.)

oblong-shaped	*rectangular*

(In American English an *oblong* is a shape much longer than it is wide and can have curved sides, e.g. a leaf.)

to take an inventory	*to take inventory*
to do a stock check	*to take stock*

Practice

1 Complete the sentences with prepositions.

a You'll find them . . . . the back . . . . the stores.

b It's 4 cm long . . . . 8.5 cm wide.

c All the moving parts are made . . . . hand. That's why they're so expensive.

d What's this used . . . . ?

e It's made . . . . rubber.

f They are manufactured . . . . our sister company.

g It's 3.5 m . . . . diameter.

2 Choose the correct form of the word in brackets.

EXAMPLE: You need to . . widen . . . . it by another two metres. (wide)

a How . . . . is the tank? (wide)

b What's the . . . . of the room? (wide)

c How . . . . is the axle? (long)

d Can you . . . . this workbench? (long)

e I think we need to adjust the . . . . of the shelves. (long)

f Do you know how . . . . the reservoir is? (deep)

g Please make sure the tank is the correct . . . . (deep)

h I can't reach that shelf. It's too . . . . (high)

i We might need to increase the . . . . of the new shed. (high)

3 Complete the sentences using a word from the box below.

loosen	tape	stored	round
workbench	check	~~stock~~	facilities

EXAMPLE: I'm afraid we don't have that item in . . stock . . . .

a That makes a total of 59 897 tonnes. Say, 60 000 tonnes if we . . . . it up to the nearest thousand.

b Please don't take anything from the stores room today. I'm trying to do a stock . . . .

c This is too tight, could you . . . . it a bit?

d Where are the chemicals . . . . ?

e The new workshop will have better . . . .

f Don't leave the tools lying on the . . . . ! Put them away.

g Have you seen my . . . . measure? I think I've lost it.

4 Picture crossword.

Use a dictionary to check the correct English terms and complete the crossword.

Across

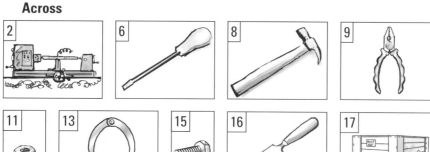

Down

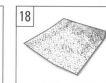
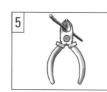
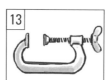

5 Match the two parts of the sentences.

1	Have you tried	a	out of stock
2	I'll order	b	by about 30 cm?
3	It's small, round and	c	new tank?
4	We carry out	d	using a pair of pliers?
5	Can you widen it	e	another one for you.
6	I'm afraid they're	f	made of plastic.
7	I can install it	g	most repairs ourselves.
8	How deep is the	h	as soon as it arrives.

6 Complete the chart.

The first one has been done as an example.

	noun	adjective	Complete the sentence
	triangle	triangular	It's shaped like a ..triangle........
			It's ....
			It's .... shaped.
			It's a ....
			It's a .... shape.
			It's ....
			It's a(n) ....

4 Suppliers and sub-contractors

Some useful phrases.
Listen to the recording and repeat.

We look for companies with a good track record.
We've built up very good relationships with our suppliers.
We tend to deal with three local companies.

At peak times we hire in casual workers.
We contract out certain services.

Our usual supplier has let us down.
I'm not happy with their response time.
We work to very low tolerance levels.

I'd like to check the terms and conditions of the contract.
It's due for renewal at the end of the month.
Is it still under guarantee?

We recommend you take out an extended warranty.
What does that include?
It covers all parts and labour.
There's no call-out fee.
It's included in the annual service contract.

Dialogues 1

Choosing suppliers

A: How do you choose which companies to work with?

B: Well, there are lots of things to consider. Quality and delivery times are as important as price. We also take into consideration technical support and after-sales service. **We look for companies with a good track record.** We place a few trial orders and if everything goes well, we put them on our approved list. It's important to choose companies you feel you can work closely with.

Guaranteed supply

A: Quality is very important to us. **We work to very low tolerance levels.** We need to have guaranteed supplies of consistently high quality raw materials. Over the years **we've built up very good relationships with our suppliers.**

B: Do you have many different suppliers?

A: Yes. **There are about fifty names on our approved supplier list,** but for raw materials **we tend to deal with three local companies.**

Extra staff

A: I was surprised to see how few people you have on-site. You provide a wide range of goods and services but have a very small workforce.

B: It depends on the time of year. **At peak times we hire in casual workers** to help with packing and dispatch. **We also contract out certain services** all year round, for example, cleaning. We run a very tight operation!

A: Do you handle the recruiting yourselves?

B: Sometimes we use a local employment agency. It depends on the job.

A new supplier

A: Hi Steve. What do you think of the new supplier?

B: We haven't had any problems so far. They offer a 24-hour technical back-up service. We've called them in three times this month. **They always arrive within a couple of hours.**

A: That's good service. Do we have to pay extra for that?

B: No. **There's no call-out fee. It's included in the annual service contract.**

A rush order

A: **Our usual supplier has let us down** and I've been looking through your parts catalogue. I need fifty GT670s. **How soon can you deliver?**

B: Just a moment and I'll check. We're expecting a delivery on Friday. We've only got ten in stock at the moment. I can deliver those **by first thing tomorrow morning. There'll be an extra charge for special delivery.** I'll have to **send them by courier.**

Notes

We look for companies with a good track record.

> Similar expressions:
> *We only use suppliers with a good reputation.*
> *All our suppliers have a good name.*

We work to very low tolerance levels.

> We could also say:
> *We operate within very tight limits.*

... we've built up very good relationships with our suppliers.

> *We've established good relations* can also be used, but is more formal.

There are about fifty names on our approved supplier list, ...

> Note the use of the adjective *approved*. The noun is *approval*.
> *The Managing Director gave the project his approval.*
> The verb *approve* is followed by the preposition *of:*
> *I don't approve of the new system.*

... we tend to deal with three local companies.

> Note the preposition *with* after deal.
> Similar expressions:
> *We do most of our business with ...*
> *We source most of our materials from ...*
> *Tend to/have a tendency to* means *this is normally the case.*
> Look at the following example:
> *Prices tend to go up at this time of year.*

At peak times we hire in casual workers ...

> *peak times* are busy periods.
> *Traffic is very heavy during peak hours.*
> Instead of *hire in* we could also say *bring in, take on* or *employ.*
> *We've taken on a new Transport Manager.*

We also contract out certain services ...

> We could also say...
> *We buy in certain services.*
> A company or person providing a service over a period of time is called a *sub-contractor* or just a *contractor*.

They always arrive within a couple of hours.

> *Within* means it will be a couple of hours at the most.

There's no call-out fee. It's included in the annual service contract.

> A *call-out fee* is often charged in addition to the cost of repair.

Our usual supplier has let us down ...

> If you *let someone down* you don't keep your promise or do as agreed.

How soon can you deliver?

> We could also say:
> *How quickly can you get the goods here?*

... by first thing tomorrow morning.

> Note the use of *by* for a deadline.
> *We must have it by Monday.*
> *first thing tomorrow morning* means at the start of the working day.

There'll be an extra charge for special delivery.

> Extra charges are also called *supplements* or *surcharges*.

... send them by courier.

> Note the preposition *by* for types of transport: *by airfreight; by rail; by road*

British/American differences

British	American
We work to very low tolerance levels. (not used in American English)	Similar to *We work to exacting standards.*
We hire in casual workers	*We hire temporary workers*
There's no call-out fee.	*There's no house-call/ travel time/ service call fee.*
catalogue	*catalog*
Managing Director	*Chief Executive Officer*
We source most of our materials from ...	*We get/obtain/ purchase/ buy most of our materials from ...* (also used in British English)
Transport Manager	*Transportation Manager*

Dialogues 2

A service contract

A: Do you have a copy of our service contract with Telecoms? **I'm not happy with their response time** and **I'd like to check the terms and conditions of the contract.**

B: Sure. I've got a copy here. **It's due for renewal at the end of next month.** We've still got time to look for another supplier if you're not happy.

Extended warranty

A: How long have we had the A3 printer in the sales department?

B: Just over a year I think. Why, what's the problem?

A: I'm not sure but there seems to be something wrong with it. **Is it still under guarantee?**

B: I think **the guarantee's just run out.** Let me check. Oh, it's OK. **We took out an extended warranty. It runs until next March.**

A product guarantee

A: Can you tell me what's included in your warranty?

B: Certainly. The product has a two-year guarantee. If it breaks down during that period we offer a replacement unit completely **free of charge.** Our products are very reliable but **we recommend you take out** an extended warranty. This covers you for a further two years.

A: I see. **What does that include?**

B: It covers all parts and labour, except for normal wear and tear of course.

A: What sort of response time do you guarantee?

B: **Our engineers are on call 24 hours a day**. We guarantee someone will be with you within four hours, but in practice it's often much sooner.

A: **Are there any exclusions?**

B: Not really. **It's a very comprehensive warranty.** I'll put a copy in the post to you and you can **read through the small print.**

An insurance policy

A: Bad news, I'm afraid. **Our supplier has gone bust.** The parts you ordered have arrived at the docks but the handling agent won't release them until someone pays the invoice. We also need to arrange transport to the factory.

B: Don't worry about the cost. **Our insurance policy covers us against situations like this.** We need those parts urgently. Could you please try to get them here tomorrow?

Notes

I'm not happy with their response time ...

Similar expressions:

I'm dissatisfied with their turnaround time.

They don't respond promptly.

... I'd like to check the terms and conditions of the contract.

terms and conditions is a common expression for the details of a contract or agreement.

It's due for renewal at the end of next month.

Other expressions:

The contract expires tomorrow.

It runs out next week.

We need to renew the contract soon.

Is it still under guarantee?

We could also say:

Is the guarantee still valid?

Has the guarantee expired yet?

... the guarantee's just run out.

Note the use of *run out* to mean *expired/is no longer valid.*

Guarantee is also used as a verb.

It is guaranteed for two years.

We took out an extended warranty.

take out means arrange and pay for.

We decided not to take out fully comprehensive cover.

It runs until next March.

Note the use of *until*. Other examples:

The contractors will be here until the end of the year.

We can't pay the hauliers until we have received the goods.

... free of charge.

This means at no extra cost.

... we recommend you take out ...

Note the verb pattern with *recommend*.

The safety inspector recommended (that) we shut down the plant.

What does that include?

We can also say:

What does the policy cover?

Our engineers are on call 24 hours a day.

If you are *on call*, you are ready to come into work if necessary.

Are there any exclusions?

An *exclusion* is an exception, a situation which is not covered by the policy.

It's a very comprehensive warranty.

A *comprehensive warranty* has few exclusions.

... read through the small print.

The *small print* is the list of conditions and exclusions of a contract or agreement.

Our supplier has gone bust.

This means the company has gone out of business, is bankrupt.

Our insurance policy covers us against situations like this.

This means the supplier/insurance company will pay for new or replacement components and for fitting or repair. Other examples of *cover*.

The policy doesn't cover wear and tear.

We're covered against fire and theft.

Are you sure we're covered against accidental damage?

We need comprehensive cover for all goods in transit.

British/American differences

British	American
A3, A4 (these paper sizes are not used in American English.)	Standard paper is *legal size* (14″x 8½″) and letter size (11″x 8½″).
labour	*labor*
in the post	*in the mail*
arrange transport to the factory	*arrange transportation to the factory*
hauliers	*haulers*

Practice

1 Complete the sentences with a preposition.

a   The guarantee is valid . .for. . . . . . . three years.

b   If it breaks down, we will replace it free . . . . charge.

c   We can provide a new unit . . . . no extra cost.

d   We guarantee delivery . . . . three working days.

e   We buy . . . . certain services when we're busy.

f   We have decided not to take . . . . the extended warranty.

g   Is the unit still . . . . guarantee?

h   We've built . . . . very good relationships with our suppliers.

i   We don't deal . . . . that supplier any more.

2 Match the two parts of the sentences.

1	Are we covered	a	small workforce.
2	I'm glad we took out	b	due for renewal.
3	The service contract is	c	to break down quite often.
4	The policy doesn't provide cover against	d	for accidental damage?
5	We have a very	e	theft.
6	The packing machine tends	f	an extended warranty.

3 Complete the sentences using the words from the box below.

services	charge	suppliers	deliver	tolerance	bust	deal
peak	reputation	conditions	comprehensive	approved		

EXAMPLE: If we don't . .deliver. . this order on time, we will lose the contract.

a   We're thinking of changing our raw material . . . .

b   It's a very . . . . warranty. It covers everything.

c   I work in the Lab. I don't usually . . . . with our customers directly.

d   We supply a wide range of goods and . . . .

e   We operate to very tight . . . . levels.

f   It's important to have a good . . . . in business.

g   Is the company on our . . . . list?

h   We're very busy at the moment. It's one of our . . . . times.

i   I've just heard that our main supplier has gone . . . .

j   Are you sure you've read the terms and . . . . carefully?

k   We guarantee to replace it free of . . . .

4 Choose the correct time preposition

EXAMPLE: The guarantee is valid *until (for) by* three years.

a The warranty runs out *within / in / until* September.

b It's due for renewal *at / on / in* the beginning of the month.

c The guarantee runs *for / until / in* next June.

d We must have that part *on / by / in* next Friday.

e If the machine breaks down *on / during / for* the guarantee period, we offer an immediate replacement.

f We guarantee delivery *for / by / within* three working days.

g We usually take on extra fitters *on / within / at* peak times.

h We can't deliver the part *until / on / during* next Monday.

i If the job is urgent, we will get to you *for / during / within* a couple of hours.

5 Match the two parts of the expressions.

wear		conditions
parts		tear
goods	and	maintenance
terms		labour
repair		services

6 Put the verb in brackets into the correct form.

EXAMPLE: We're expecting ...... (expect) another delivery on Friday.

a We . . . . (build up) good relationships over the past few years.

b Have you heard the news? Our suppliers . . . . (go bust).

c The contract . . . . (run out) tomorrow.

d Our engineers . . . . (be) always on call 24 hours a day.

e I . . . . (put) a copy of the contract in the post to you tomorrow.

f When we're busy, we . . . . (hire in) casual workers.

g There . . . . (seem) to be something wrong with my laptop.

7 Write a suitable question for each answer. Refer to the dialogues and notes.

EXAMPLE: Have ..you contracted out any of your services........?

Yes, we've contracted out all our cleaning and catering services.

a Is ....?

No, it's just run out.

b Do ....?

No, we use a local employment agency.

c Do ....?

Yes, there are about thirty on our approved list.

d How ....?

We can deliver the order by the end of the week.

e When ....?

At the end of the month. Shall we renew it, or look for another supplier?

f What ....?

It covers you for fire, theft and accidental damage, but not wear and tear.

g How ....?

It's valid for three years from date of purchase.

h Are there ....?

Not really. It's a very comprehensive warranty.

i Do we ....?

No, there's no call-out fee. It's included in the contract.

j What ....?

It includes all parts and labour.

5 Buildings and installations

Some useful phrases.
Listen to the recording and repeat.

When is the building work due to start?
It'll take three weeks to demolish the old building.
How long will the sub-contractors be on site?

It must be ready on time.
The first phase of the project was finished three days ahead of schedule.
We're on target to complete phase two.

We've had a slight delay.
We're working to a really tight schedule.
We can still meet the deadline.

How long will the system be down for?
We've allowed forty-eight hours to be on the safe side.
The program's going live on Monday.

The crew is on stand-by.
We've taken on a civil engineer.

Dialogues 1

A new warehouse

A: Here are the plans for the new finished goods warehouse. Do you have any thoughts or comments?

B: I think the plans look good. There's just one thing though. **I'm a bit concerned about** the main lorry entrance. **What's the height clearance?**

A: Let me check. It's 3.80 m.

B: Are you sure that's high enough?

A: **That's a good point.** I'll make a note to increase it to 4.80 to make sure we can accept the new containers.

The building schedule

A: I see there are some workmen on the site. **When is the building work due to start?**

B: Well, **it'll take three weeks to demolish the old building** and **clear away the debris.** We should be ready to start the construction work in week 23.

A: **How long will the sub-contractors be on site?**

B: About ten weeks in total **if everything goes according to plan.**

A: I'm sure it will. So, we should be able to start moving the machinery in during week 34. I'll confirm that date with our suppliers.

Project planning

A: Who's in charge of the construction project?

B: **We've taken on a civil engineer** **on a nine-month temporary contract.** He'll oversee the whole project. In fact we're having a project meeting at 3 p.m this afternoon **to allocate responsibilities** and finalise the time schedule. Why don't you join us?

A: I can't I'm afraid. I've got another meeting scheduled for 2:30 p.m.

Making progress

A: How's the building work going?

B: Well, I'm afraid **we've had a slight delay.**

A: What's the problem? We really can't have any delays at this stage. **We're working to a really tight schedule** and we're already **over budget.**

B: The cement arrived late but don't worry, I'm confident **we can still meet the deadline.** **The crew is on stand-by** and as soon as the concrete has set we can get started again.

A: OK. Keep me informed. **It must be ready on time.**

Notes

I'm a bit concerned about ...
> We could also say:
> *I have some concerns about ...*
> *I'm a little worried about ...*

What's the height clearance?
> *clearance* is used to describe the distance from the ground to the top of an entrance/roof/bridge.

That's a good point.
> A useful way of showing you agree with what someone has said.

When is the building work due to start?
> Note the use of *due*. An alternative expression:
> *When is it scheduled to start?*

... it'll take three weeks to demolish the old building ...
> *demolish* means *knock down*.
> Note the use of *it'll take* for the amount of time needed.
> *It'll take two hours to repair the generator.*
> *We need twenty-four hours for the concrete to set.*

... clear away the debris.
> *debris* is another word for rubbish.

How long will the sub-contractors be on site?
> *on site* means in the company grounds and/or buildings.

... if everything goes according to plan.
> We could also say:
> *If everything goes as planned.*
> *If we can keep to our schedule.*

We've taken on a civil engineer ...
> We could also say:
> *We've recruited/hired/brought in a ...*

... on a nine-month temporary contract.
> Other expressions:
> *on a temporary basis*
> *temporarily*
> The opposite of *temporary* is *permanent*.

... to allocate responsibilities ...
> This means to decide who is going to be responsible for certain duties.

... we've had a slight delay.
> *slight* means *minor* or *small*.
> Other expressions:
> *I'm afraid we've got a slight problem.*
> *There's been a slight change of plan.*

We're working to a really tight schedule ...
> Another expression with *tight*:
> *I hope the parts arrive in time. It's going to be very tight.* (This means we have very little time.)

... over budget.
> When discussing finance *over budget* means something cost more than planned.

... we can still meet the deadline.
> This means that you manage to do the work by the date/time agreed.

The crew is on stand-by ...
> If you are on *stand-by*, you are ready to start work if needed.

It must be ready on time.
> Note we don't use *to* after *must*.
> *The delivery must arrive on time.*
> Note: **NOT** *The delivery must to arrive on time.*

British/American differences

British	American
I'm a bit concerned	I'm a little concerned

(The words *bit* and *little* can be used in both British and American English, but would not be used in this context. For example, *I'm a bit concerned* is a very British expression and would not be used in American English in this way.)

British	American
rubbish	garbage
finalise	finalize

Dialogues 2

Phase 1 of a project

A: Hi, Paulo. How are things going?

B: Everything's going very well. **The first phase of the project** was finished **three days ahead of schedule. We're on target to complete phase two** by the beginning of week 40.

A: That's good news. What stage are you at now?

B: Well, we've just finished laying the cabling and we're waiting for the safety inspector to **give us the go-ahead to continue.** I'm just going to meet him. Do you want to come?

A new stock system

A: Is the new computerised stock system **in operation?**

B: Not quite. The software engineers are testing it just now.

A: Have all the operators been trained on it?

B: Yes, most of them. **We trained on a dummy system** last month. A couple of people were away so we've organised two more training sessions on **the live system** for the whole team this week.

Going live

A: **Our new production control program's going live on Monday.** The old and **the new programs will operate in tandem** for four to six weeks. That should give us time to **iron out any little problems.**

B: Hope it all goes well. We're very busy at the moment and certainly don't want any problems at this time of year.

A: Yes, I realise that. We've spent a long time planning and preparing for the change-over. I'm confident we won't have any major problems.

An upgrade

A: We need to take the accounts system offline to carry out the upgrade. But don't worry, it won't cause too much inconvenience. We're going to do it over the weekend.

B: **How long will the system be down for?**

A: We'll be taking everything offline **in about two hours' time.** It'll be down **for a minimum of twelve hours.** If everything goes according to plan, it should be up again by 6 pm on Saturday.

B: That's fine. **We've allowed forty-eight hours to be on the safe side.**

Notes

The first phase of the project ...

Note the use of *phase* to describe a stage in a project.
Phase two of the building work will soon be finished.
When describing *a process* we use the word *stage*.
The first stage in the process is to remove the toxins.

... three days ahead of schedule.

This means *three days earlier than planned*.
The opposite is *behind schedule* (i.e. later than planned).
Despite the slight delay we're still on schedule to complete the project by the end of this month.
I'm sorry to inform you that the building works have fallen behind schedule.

We're on target to complete phase two ...

on target means the same as *on schedule* (see above). *Target* can also be used to describe sales or production goals.
We met our sales target last month.
Our tonnage is below target this quarter.

... give us the go-ahead to continue.

Other similar expressions:
We've got approval for the project.
I hope we get the green light.

... in operation.

A common expression which means *working*.

We trained on a dummy system ...

We could also say:
a trial system
a test platform

... the live system ...

the opposite of a *dummy system*

Our new production control program's going live on Monday.

Note the use of *going live*.
We could also say:
The system will be fully operational on Monday.

... the new programs will operate in tandem ...

in tandem means both systems will run at the same time.

... iron out any little problems.

This means to discover and solve any problems.

How long will the system be down for?

Note the use of *down*. We can also say:
How long will it be offline?

... in about two hours' time.

Note the use of *in* + a period of time to say **when** something will happen.
It will be ready in twenty minutes.
The shift is changing in half an hour.

... for a minimum for twelve hours.

We use *for* + a period of time to say **how long** something will last.
The warehouse will be out of use for three months.
Our foreman is on holiday for ten days.

We've allowed forty-eight hours to be on the safe side.

Note the use of *allow* for time.
You should allow at least one hour for the machine to cool down.
We allowed an extra two days for the machine rebuild.

British/American differences	
British	**American**
computerised	computerized
organised	organized
realise	realize
in about two hours' time	in about two hours
schedule	schedule
'ʃedʒuːl, 'skedjuːl	'skɛdʒəl, 'skɛdʒul
on holiday	on vacation

Practice

1 Complete the sentences with prepositions.

a   It is very important to arrive at the meeting . . . . time.

b   I'm happy to report we are . . . . schedule and the building will be finished
. . . . June as planned.

c   The new parts cost more than we thought. I'm afraid the project is now . . . .
budget.

d   The builders still haven't finished the new warehouse. We are three weeks . . . .
schedule and might need to find other temporary raw material storage facilities.

e   The sub-contractors will be staying on site . . . . six weeks.

f   Good news! Despite the delay, we're still . . . . target to finish the project
this week.

2 Match the two parts of the sentences.

1	Everyone has been trained	a	twenty new staff.
2	The engineer helped iron	b	meet the deadline?
3	I'm a bit concerned	c	away the debris.
4	We've taken on	d	ready to start phase two?
5	When are we going to	e	out a few problems.
6	Are the builders	f	take the network offline?
7	I hope they're going to clear	g	about the delays we've had.
8	Do you think we can still	h	on the new system.

3 Complete the sentences using *in* or *for*.

EXAMPLE: We can move into the new building . . .*in*. . . . . . . a few weeks.

a   The workshop will be out of use . . . . two days because it's being repainted.

b   The Production Manager isn't in today. She's on holiday . . . . two weeks.

c   The new offices will be ready . . . . about a week from now.

d   Starting today, the contractors will be on site . . . . ten weeks.

e   The cement should arrive . . . . the next hour or so.

4 Complete the sentences using the words from the box below.

tight	demolish	down	slight	tandem	live	allowed
~~clearance~~	testing	go-ahead	safety	installed		

EXAMPLE: Are you sure we've got enough height . clearance. . for the new trucks?

a   When two processes are operating at the same time, we say they're running
    in . . . .

b   Good news! We've got the . . . . for the new buildings.

c   We don't have any spare time. We've got a really . . . . schedule.

d   How much time have you . . . . for the cabling work?

e   How long will it take to . . . . the old factory?

f   The . . . . inspector has condemned this warehouse.

g   I'm afraid there's been a . . . . delay.

h   The anti-virus software was . . . . last week.

i   When do you think the new computer system will go . . . . ?

j   How much longer do you think the network will be . . . . for?

k   The engineers are . . . . the phone lines at the moment.

5 Complete the sentences using the correct form of the verb in brackets.

EXAMPLE: The engineers . are testing . (test) the system at the moment.

a   The delivery must . . . . (arrive) on time.

b   We're on target . . . . (complete) the project ahead of schedule.

c   It'll take three weeks, if everything . . . . (go) according to plan.

d   Everyone . . . . (be) very busy at the moment.

e   I hope we can . . . . (meet) the deadline.

f   How much time have you . . . . (allow) to clear the site?

g   We . . . . (finish) phase two of the project last week.

h   When . . . . (be) the new system due to go into operation?

6 Write down a suitable question for the following answers.

EXAMPLE: How ...long will the sub-contractors be on site............ ?

About ten weeks in total.

a How .... ?

Very well. We're ahead of schedule.

b Is .... ?

It's not quite ready. The software engineers are testing it now.

c How .... ?

It'll be down for about thirty minutes.

d What .... ?

We've just finished phase one and are ready to start phase two.

e What .... ?

It's 4.80 m. – high enough for our lorries.

7 Rearrange the letters to form a word used in the dialogues, then match the word to its definition.

EXAMPLE: srebid	debris	a opposite of temporary
1 smloedih		b approval or permission to continue
2 brt-scctusroona		c time or date when something must be finished
3 neatenrpm		d ready to work if needed
4 eldeandi		e knock down a building
5 efoaegnr reiwstne		f working (a machine or system)
6 da-heoga		g rubbish or waste material
7 rp toaninioe		h a person who writes or fixes computer programs
8 sa ndynotb		i people from another company employed for a specific job

6 Maintenance

Someone has reported a fault.

This model's designed for heavy use.
It's usually very reliable.

I'd like to go over the list of jobs.
We might need to extend the shut.

We need to reduce our downtime.
There have been too many unplanned shutdowns.
We need to establish routine maintenance procedures.

It's a crucial part of our process.
We try to replace components before they fail or wear out.

When was it serviced?
How often do you service the vans?
We can give the engines a major overhaul.
We strip down the engine and replace the faulty component.

Dialogues 1

A minor fault

A: Hi. Someone has reported a fault on one of your copiers.

B: That's right. I'm glad you're here. It hasn't been working properly for the last few days.

A: When was it serviced?

B: Just a couple of weeks ago. It's usually very reliable.

A: What's actually wrong with it?

B: Well, it's making a strange noise when we try to change paper trays.

A: I'm sure it's nothing serious, probably just a minor fault. I'll have a look at it.

Light or heavy use?

A: I've just got a new printer. How often do I need to replace the print heads?

B: Well, under normal conditions each head lasts about 5 000 copies or so. It depends on the user, but about once a month is average.

A: So if I don't print out very much, it could last a lot longer?

B: That's right. It could last six months or more. This model's designed for heavy use. Don't worry – you'll get an error message telling you when to change the head.

Common problems

A: What sort of problems do you have with these machines?

B: They're quite complex machines and they have a lot of different components. We need to check the metal casing regularly for any signs of corrosion. We also check the brushes once a fortnight to make sure they aren't worn down. It's important to make sure everything is properly aligned and we adjust it if necessary. There is a canvas belt at the end of the assembly line. If it gets wet, it might rot so we check that regularly too.

Jobs to do

A: Hi, Xavier. I'd like to go over the list of jobs for next week's maintenance shut.

B: Sure. We've got a lot to do in a short time. We're planning to shut the line at midday on Wednesday and start up again at 6 pm the following day. We might need to extend the shut by about six hours.

A: Our production people won't be happy about that. We've got a full order book at the moment. Is there any way you could speed things up?

B: Not really. We need to dismantle the conveyor belt and replace the rollers.

Notes

Someone has reported a fault ...
> Note the expression to *report a fault*.

When was it serviced?
> *service* is a noun and a verb. Note the
> following expressions:
> *It is serviced regularly.*
> *We carry out regular services.*

It's usually very reliable.
> The opposite is *unreliable*.
> Other expressions:
> *We rarely have any problems with it.*
> *It generally runs very smoothly.*

... a minor fault.
> *minor* means small/unimportant
> the opposite is *major* or a *serious fault*.

I'll have a look at it.
> Note the preposition *at*. We can also say
> *I'll check it*.

... each head lasts about 5 000 copies or so.
> *or so* means *approximately*.
> Other ways of commenting on how long
> something lasts:
> *We get about 50 000 print runs out of it.*
> *We can use it approximately 150 times.*
> *We expect around 200 hours' running time.*

This model's designed for heavy use.
> The opposite of *heavy use* is *light use*
> *It is only designed for light use.*

... complex machines ...
> A *complex machine* has many parts.
> The opposite is *simple* or *basic*.

... once a fortnight ...
> A *fortnight* is a period of two weeks.
> We could also say:
> *once every two weeks.*
> *every other week.*

... assembly line.
> An *assembly line* is a production line where
> products are put together from different
> parts.

I'd like to go over the list of jobs ...
> *go over* means *look at and discuss*.
> We can also say *go through*:
> *I'd like to go through the new procedures*
> *with you.*

... at midday on Wednesday ...
> Note the use of prepositions:
> *at* with time, *on* for days
> *at 2:30 p.m/at 18:30*
> *on Thursday/on Saturday*
> *in the morning/afternoon/evening*
> *in January/February*

We might need to extend the shut ...
> *extend* means *make longer*.
> *shut* is a common expression for a
> production shutdown.

... by about six hours.
> Note this use of *by*:
> *I need to extend the meeting by one hour.*
> *We've increased production by twenty per cent.*

We've got a full order book ...
> If talking about production capacity, we can
> also say:
> *We're fully booked.*

... speed things up.
> This means *do something faster*. The opposite
> is *slow things down*.

Dialogues 2

Preventive maintenance

A: **There have been too many unplanned shutdowns** over the past few months. We'll have to make a few changes to the way we operate. **We need to reduce our downtime.**

B: I agree, but **the maintenance team is fully stretched** dealing with problems. We don't have time to carry out any preventive maintenance.

A: **We need to establish routine maintenance procedures.** It costs us too much in lost production if we wait until something breaks down before we fix it.

Discussing frequency

A: How often do you service the pump?

B: We take very good care of this particular pump. **It's a crucial part of our process.** We clean it and **flush it through** at the end of every shift. We check the high pressure seals, **recalibrate the gauges** and lubricate all moving parts weekly. We replace the gaskets every month.

A: How do you decide how often these things need to be done?

B: Well, from experience **we can predict the lifespan** of different components. **We try to replace components before they fail or wear out.** This prevents the equipment from breaking down. It also saves us a lot of trouble!

Regular services

A: This is our main service area. We do all the routine services here and have two full-time mechanics.

B: **How often do you service the vans?**

A: They're serviced regularly. We give them **a basic service every 10 000 km or so** and a main service once a year, or every 100 000 km.

B: I see. What does the service involve?

A: Well, the same as for private vehicles really, but we do it more often because **they get a lot of wear and tear.**

B: Can you carry out major repairs here?

A: Yes, we've got all the necessary equipment. We can **give the engines a major overhaul.** If there's a serious problem, **we strip down the engine and find the faulty component.** Would you like to look around?

Non-urgent repairs

A: What do you do if you find something that isn't on your list?

B: It depends what it is. **Once we have disconnected the unit,** we do as many jobs as we can. If there is something that isn't broken but might cause a problem before the next service then of course we repair it or replace that part. But if it's not urgent, **we make a note in the service record** to carry out that repair next time.

Notes

There have been too many unplanned shutdowns ...

> Note the use of the prefix *un* to mean *not*.
> Other examples:
> *Our vans run on unleaded petrol*
> *We need to unblock the pipe.*

We need to reduce our downtime.

> *Downtime* is when the production line is shut because of a problem.

... the maintenance team is fully stretched ...

> *Fully stretched* means *working at full capacity* and unable to do any more work.

We need to establish routine maintenance procedures.

> Note the use of *establish*.
> We could also say *set up*.
> *They are going to set up a preventive maintenance schedule.*

It's a crucial part of our process.

> *crucial* means *essential, vital*.

... flush it through ...

> *flush* means to pass a lot of water or liquid through a pipe, usually to clean it.

... recalibrate the gauges ...

> Note the use of the prefix *re* to mean *again*.
> Other examples:
> *I've reset the levels.*
> *We're ready to re-assemble the unit.*
> *We can re-use it. Don't throw it out.*

... we can predict the lifespan ...

> *lifespan* is how long a component or piece of equipment will work.

We try to replace components before they fail or wear out.

> If a component or machine *fails,* it breaks down. The noun is *failure.*
> *Our communication system has failed.*
> *There's been a power failure.*

How often do you service the vans?

> This is the most common way of asking about frequency. Note how to reply:
> *The filters are changed monthly.*
> *We test the system on a regular basis.*
> *We carry out a full diagnostic test twice a month.*

... a basic service every 10 000 km or so ...

> Note the use of *every*:
> *We replace the bulbs every month.*
> *It has to be changed every 100 hours.*

... they get a lot of wear and tear.

> *wear and tear* is damage which happens when something is used a lot.

... give the engines a major overhaul.

> *An overhaul* is a detailed service.

... we strip down the engine and find the faulty component.

> *strip down* means *dismantle* or *take apart*.
> Another example:
> *We'll need to strip down the assembly line to replace the faulty part.*

Once we have disconnected the unit, ...

> *disconnect* means *undo the connection.* Other examples with *dis*:
> *Make sure the gears are disengaged.*
> *Disengaged* means not in position.
> *Something has dislodged the bearing.*
> *Dislodged* means moved it from its position.

... we make a note in the service record ...

> We could also say:
> *Write it down in the service log.*

British/American differences	
British	**American**
petrol	gas(oline)

Practice

1 Choose the correct verb *make* or *do*.

EXAMPLE: We ... *do* ...... the routine services on-site.

a We've got a lot of work to .... before the end of the month.

b I think we need to .... a few changes to our document management procedures.

c Does that engine always .... a strange noise?

d Will you have enough time to .... all the jobs on your list?

e Could you .... a note to order a replacement unit?

2 Match an expression in column A with one in column B.

A	B
often	annually
every two weeks	weekly
hardly ever	frequently
once a year	once a day
every week	rarely
on a daily basis	fortnightly

3 Match the two parts of the sentences.

1	We need to carry out	a	the component fails.
2	How often	b	regular backups.
3	I phoned the engineer to	c	some more time to complete all the repairs.
4	We don't wait until	d	some routine maintenance tasks.
5	It's important to take	e	do you do a diagnostic test?
6	We might need	f	report a fault.

4 Complete the sentences with a preposition.

a It's not designed .... heavy use.

b It's a very durable system. .... normal operating conditions it will last many years.

c Do you know what's wrong .... it?

d Can you look .... this pump? I don't think it's working properly.

e We're going to shut the line .... midday.

f The unit will be replaced .... January.

g It's a crucial part .... our process.

h The electrician will be here .... Tuesday.

5 Match the two parts of the verbs and put them in the correct sentences. You might need to change the verb form.

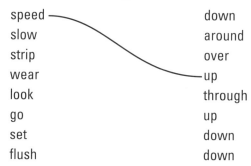

speed	down
slow	around
strip	over
wear	up
look	through
go	up
set	down
flush	down

EXAMPLE: We need to finish this job by Friday. We'd better . speed up . . . . . .

a   First . . . . the engine and then clean all the parts.

b   We need to replace the roller brushes; they've . . . .

c   Would you like me to . . . . the job list with you?

d   Don't forget to . . . . the pipes . . . . with clean water.

e   The safety inspector is going to . . . . the site.

f   We're going to . . . . a new system for reporting faults.

g   We need to . . . . the rotor. It's turning too fast.

6 Complete the sentences using the words from the box below.

~~smoothly~~	moving	often
capacity	dismantle	essential

EXAMPLE: The engine has been running very . . smoothly . . . . since its last service.

a   This is an . . . . part of our manufacturing process.

b   Remember to lubricate all . . . . parts.

c   We can't accept any more orders for next month. We're already working at full
. . . .

d   How . . . . do you check the machine settings?

e   I'm not sure how to . . . . this section of the machine. I'll need to check the maintenance manual.

7 Choose the correct prefix – *un, re* or *dis*.

EXAMPLE: Once the liquid has cooled, we ... *re* heat it to forty degrees.

a   Sorry about the delay. We had an ...... expected problem.

b   Don't forget to ...... calibrate the sensors before you switch the power on.

c   Who left this door ...... locked?

d   There's a mistake in the maintenance schedule. Could you ...... print it, please?

e   Something has ...... lodged the sensor.

f   You must ...... connect the electricity supply before opening the casing.

g   Most cars now run on ...... leaded petrol.

h   We need to ...... order these parts.

i   Remember to ...... engage the gears before starting the engine.

8 Match the material with the problem. Use a dictionary if necessary.

1	The rubber ring	a	has broken down.
2	The brushes	b	has corroded.
3	The canvas belt	c	have worn down.
4	The component	d	has perished.
5	The metal casing	e	has rotted.
6	The engine	f	has failed.

9 Using as many of the verbs as possible, make a list of the tasks done during maintenance.

recalibrate	drain	check	top up	lubricate
clean	dismantle	replace	service	

EXAMPLE:

a   clean drain check service dismantle   a pump

b   ....   a filter

c   ....   the bearings

d   ....   a seal

e   ....   the fluid levels

f   ....   the sensors

7 Troubleshooting

Some useful phrases.
Listen to the recording and repeat.

Johan hasn't turned up.
We're very short-staffed.
Tommi can stand in for an hour.

What's wrong with the photocopier?
Have you checked the fuse?
The toner has run out.

The gears have seized up.
You'll have to dismantle the unit.

I've been having problems getting onto the Internet.
Why don't you call the Help Desk?

The system keeps crashing.
You'll need to reboot your machine.
When did you last take a backup?

The server might be down.
I might have the wrong version.
You'll have to upgrade.

◎ Dialogues 1

A personnel problem

A: Johan hasn't turned up and Stefan is ill. Do we have anyone on stand-by?

B: I'm afraid not, we're very short-staffed at the moment. Can you ask the shift supervisor to ask one of his team to do some overtime? Perhaps Tommi can stand in for an hour or two until we find a replacement.

An electrical problem

A: What's wrong?

B: There's no power.

A: Have you checked the fuse box?

B: Yes, the fuse had blown and I've changed it but now the motor keeps cutting out.

A: There might be a loose connection somewhere that's making the safety switch trip. Check the settings on the trip-switch. If you can't fix it yourself, call in an electrician.

A problem in the office

A: What's wrong with the photocopier?

B: The toner has run out and there's none in the stationery cupboard.

A: I need to make six copies of this report for the Board Meeting tomorrow. Ring Office Supplies and ask if they have any in stock. If they can't deliver this afternoon, I'll go and collect it.

Mechanical problem 1

A: What's happened? Is there a problem?

B: I think the gears have seized up.

A: You'll have to dismantle the unit and lubricate the bearings. Do it as quickly as you can but make sure you top up the oil before you start the motor up again.

Mechanical problem 2

A: Why have you stopped production?

B: We've had a few problems. One of the bolts has worked loose and a blade has snapped off.

A: OK. Make sure the power is switched off then tighten up all the bolts on the unit and replace the broken blade. Why is there oil all over the floor?

B: I think the valve is faulty. I couldn't regulate the pressure and the seal burst. I tried opening the emergency valve but it was jammed.

A: Clean up the mess first, then fit a new seal and check the valve.

Notes

Johan hasn't turned up ...

This means he hasn't arrived. We could also say:

He hasn't come in today.
He's off sick.

... on stand-by.

If someone is not actually working but is ready to work, we say they are *on stand-by*. We can also say *on call*.

I won't be able to relax properly this weekend. I'm on call.

... we're very short-staffed ...

short-staffed means *we don't have enough staff*.

We could also say:
We're short of staff.
We're short of resources.
Note: **NOT** *short-resourced*.

... Tommi can stand in for an hour ...

Stand in for means *temporarily replace* (a colleague).

Can you stand in for me when I go on holiday?

Have you checked the fuse box?

We can also say:
Have you inspected/examined/looked at ...

... the fuse had blown ...

When a fuse breaks we say it *blows*. Note also:

It has fused.

Check the settings on the trip-switch.

A *trip-switch* is a mechanical switch which turns something on or off. It is often a *safety device*.

When a *safety cut-out* **trips**, it shuts down the power.

The safety cut-out has tripped.
The switch has tripped.

What's wrong with the photocopier?

Other ways of asking what the problem is:
What's the matter with it?
What's happened to it?

The toner has run out ...

We use *run out* to say there is none left.
The new building isn't finished yet because the company has run out of money.

... the gears have seized up.

When moving machine parts get *stuck* and can't move we say they *seize up*. We can also say that something is/has *jammed*.
I can't move this lever. It's jammed.

You'll have to dismantle the unit ...

You'll have to + infinitive is a useful way of telling someone what to do when troubleshooting:
You'll have to ask for help.
You'll have to call in a specialist.
Dismantle means to take something apart so that it is in several pieces.
The opposite is to *assemble*.

I think the valve is faulty.

faulty means *not working properly*.

I couldn't regulate the pressure ...

regulate means *control*.
This valve regulates the flow of water.

... the seal burst.

If a seal *tears,* we say it *bursts*.

British/American differences	
British	**American**
When a safety cut-out trips.	*When a circuit breaker trips.*

Dialogues 2

A computer virus

A: I think I've got a virus on my computer. **Do you know how to get rid of it?** I haven't had one before.

B: I'm afraid not. **Why don't you call the Help Desk?** Someone there will be able to help you.

A: Have you got the number? I'll call them right now.

The wrong software

A: I can't open this email attachment our Paris office has sent me.

B: Are you sure you're using the right program?

A: Well, yes it's definitely the same program but **I might have the wrong version.** Their system is newer than ours.

B: That's why you can't open it. **You'll have to upgrade** before you can read the file.

The screen is frozen

A: Can you help me? The program is not responding and I don't know what to do.

B: Look at the icon in the bottom corner of your screen. Is it flashing?

A: No. It isn't.

B: OK. Try closing down all the files you're not using at the moment.

A: But I can't move the cursor at all. **My screen is frozen.** What should I do?

B: **Have you tried pressing the Escape key?**

A: Yes, but nothing's happened.

B: OK, **you'll need to reboot your machine.** Press Control, Alt and Delete at the same time.

A I've never done that before. Will I lose all my files?

B You might lose the file you were working on, but don't worry, the help desk can restore it. **When did you last take a backup?**

Internet problems

A: **I've been having problems getting onto the Internet.**

B: Have you checked your connection settings?

A: Yes, they're fine. I suppose **the server might be down** again.

B: Yes, there have been a few problems recently. Why don't you call the IT department?

Memory problems

A: **The system keeps crashing** when I try to access the personnel database.

B: I think the file is too big. You'll need to expand your memory. First, close down all the files you have open, and then …

Notes

Do you know how to get rid of it?

In computing *get rid of* means *delete*. We can also say:

How do I delete it?

Can you tell me how to delete it?

Why don't you call the Help Desk?

There are many different ways of giving advice:

You should save your work regularly.

I think you should ask an expert.

... I might have the wrong version.

Some other ways of saying what you think is *wrong*:

I suppose the server might be down.

You could have a virus on your system.

The program could be faulty.

I think there's a malfunction.

You'll have to upgrade ...

If you *upgrade* a computer program or system, you get a better, more up-to-date one.

My screen is frozen.

In computing *frozen* means *locked, unable to move.*

Have you tried pressing the Escape key?

This is another useful way of giving advice. Note the use of *try + -ing.*

Try holding down the Control key.

Have you tried saving it in a lower version?

... you'll need to reboot your machine.

You'll need to means the same as *you'll have to.*

reboot means *start your computer up again.*

Another useful expression is *a boot disk*. This means a *start-up disk.*

Have you made a boot disk?

When did you last take a backup?

We can also say *make a backup* (noun) or just *back up* (verb).

You should back up your files at the end of each week.

I've been having problems getting onto the Internet.

We can also say *accessing the Internet.*

Note the use of prepositions in the following examples:

What's the password to get into the system?

I can't get onto/into the network.

How do you get into the file/database?

Which folder is the report in?

It's on the hard disk/a floppy/CD ROM.

The information is in a file on my hard drive.

... the server might be down ...

We use *down* to describe a computer-controlled system which is *not in operation.*

The system keeps crashing ...

If something happens frequently, we say it *keeps happening*. Note the *-ing* form after *keep*:

Why do I keep getting this error message?

The printer keeps jamming.

British/American differences	
British	**American**
When did you last take a backup?	*When did you last run a backup?*

Practice

1 Complete the sentences with prepositions.

a   I can't get . . . . the Internet.

b   I've got a virus . . . . my computer.

c   I've been having problems getting . . . . the personnel database.

d   The file is . . . . the Accounts Folder . . . . the C drive.

e   What's wrong . . . . my computer?

f   I'll have to reorder some new ink cartridges. We're . . . . of stock at the moment.

2 The following expressions appear in the dialogues or notes. Match each verb with its preposition and complete each sentence with one of the alternatives.

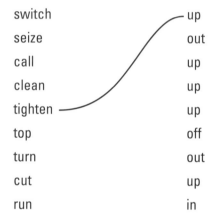

switch	up
seize	out
call	up
clean	up
tighten	up
top	off
turn	out
cut	up
run	in

EXAMPLE: Can you pass me that spanner? I need to . . tighten up . . this bolt.

a   Did you remember to . . . . the lubricating fluid after we repaired the leak?

b   We've . . . . of raw materials.

c   One of our workers didn't . . . . yesterday.

d   This workshop is very dirty. . . . . it . . . . immediately!

e   Don't forget to . . . . the power before you remove the safety guard.

f   I hope the motor doesn't . . . . again.

g   If you don't lubricate the mechanism regularly, it might . . . .

h   I think we need to . . . . an electrician.

3 Match the two parts of the sentences.

1	My computer keeps	a	rebooting the system.
2	Have you checked the	b	to replace the bearings.
3	It might	c	the toner cartridge.
4	You need	d	phone an engineer?
5	Why don't you	e	pressure?
6	I think you	f	crashing.
7	You'll have to replace	g	should check the filters.
8	Try	h	be broken.

4 Use your dictionary and complete the sentences with the most suitable word from the box.

lubricated	tripped	blown	snapped	leak	loose
crashed	expand	fault	jammed	cursor	restore

EXAMPLE: The fuse has .... blown ....

a   I think you should .... the memory.

b   My computer has ....

c   The gearing mechanism has .... again.

d   Can you help me .... the data?

e   The safety switch has ....

f   The blade has .... off.

g   My mouse isn't working, I can't move the ....

h   There has been an oil ....

i   The bolt has worked ....

j   I think there is a .... in the program.

k   Have you .... all the moving parts?

5 Complete the sentences with the correct form of the verbs in brackets.

EXAMPLE: Why don't you . .phone. . . . . (phone) the supplier?

a   You'll need to . . . . (drain) the system completely.

b   Try . . . . (adjust) the release valve.

c   I think you should . . . . (switch off) the power.

d   You'll have to . . . . (upgrade) your software.

e   Have you tried . . . . (replace) the bearings?

f   Quick, ... (close) the valve!

g   The power keeps . . . . (cut out).

6 Write down a response to the following problems. Refer to the dialogues.

EXAMPLE: I can't open this attachment.

Are you sure you're using the right program? . . . .

a   What's wrong with the photocopier?

   . . . .

b   The file is too big.

   . . . .

c   I can't move the cursor.

   . . . .

d   There's no power.

   . . . .

e   Do you know how to get rid of a virus?

   . . . .

f   The gears have seized up.

   . . . .

8 Safety in the workplace

Some useful phrases.
Listen to the recording and repeat.

You should put your ear plugs in.
You mustn't smoke here.
You must wear goggles in that area.

Mind out! Don't get too close.
Please be careful when you walk across the floor.
It might be slippery.
Make sure you know how to stop the machine.
Check that all the safety guards are fitted correctly.

Some of the materials we use are highly-flammable.
Could you just run through the evacuation procedure?
When you hear the fire alarm, go to the nearest fire exit.
Always shut the fire doors to prevent the fire spreading.

I think he's hurt his back.
What shall we do?
I'll get the first-aider.
We'd better not move him.

Dialogues 1

A noisy environment

"OK, so let's look round the factory now. **It's quite a hazardous environment** so you need to take care. By the way, **you should put your ear plugs in** when we go down to the factory. It's not compulsory but some of the machines are a bit noisy."

Warning signs

"This is the machine hall. Do you notice that sign over there – the red circle with a diagonal line through it? It means **you mustn't smoke here.** A blue circle shows something is compulsory – so that sign over there means **you must wear goggles in that area** to protect your eyes. The yellow triangle with a black border over there is a warning sign. It means the floor might be wet."

Hazards

"**Mind out. Don't get too close.** It's very hot. We don't want you to burn yourself. And **please be careful when you walk across the floor. It might be slippery.**"

"So, if you follow me into the Finished Goods Area now ... Mind you don't trip when you go past the packing area. Someone has left some wooden pallets on the floor. And be careful when you walk across the warehouse. **There might be a fork-lift truck reversing into the storage area.**"

Machine safety

"I realise **some of you are already familiar with the safety procedures** for this type of machine but I'll just explain some of the basics again. First of all, **make sure you know how to stop the machine** before you start it. That seems obvious but it's important."

"Now on this machine **always check that all the safety guards are fitted correctly** before you operate the machine because **if you don't, someone might have a bad accident.** What else? Oh yes, never try to clean a machine that's in motion. Switch it off and unplug it."

"And finally, tell your supervisor immediately if you think the machine is not working properly or if you think there are any problems. Okay, so has anyone got any questions?"

Notes

It's quite a hazardous environment ...

Something that is *hazardous* is dangerous to people's health or safety.
Note also *hazard*:
The workshop is full of hazards.

... you should put your ear plugs in ...

Should is used to show that something is recommended (but not compulsory).
Some other ways of doing this:
I recommend you put your ear plugs in.
I suggest you wear goggles in this area.

... you mustn't smoke here.

Some other ways of saying this:
You can't smoke here.
You're not allowed to smoke here.
Smoking is prohibited here.
Smoking isn't allowed here.

... you must wear goggles in that area ...

We can also say:
Goggles must be worn.
Goggles are compulsory / obligatory.

Mind out! Don't get too close.

Some other expressions with *mind* to warn someone of a possible danger:
Mind you don't trip!
Mind your head!

... please be careful when you walk across the floor.

Please be careful when ... is another way of giving a warning.

It might be slippery.

Note *might/may* indicates that something is possible. *It might/may be* is used with an adjective:
It might be hot. It may be noisy.

There might be a fork-lift truck reversing into the storage area.

There might/may be is used with a noun:
There might/may be oil on the floor.

... some of you are already familiar with the safety procedures ...

You can also say:
Some of you already know about the safety procedures.
Some of you have already been shown the safety procedures.
A *procedure* is the correct way of doing things, usually in a fixed order.

... make sure you know how to stop the machine ...

Note other ways of talking about safety regulations:
Never attempt to clean a machine that's in motion.
Tell your supervisor immediately.
Check that the area around the machine is clean and tidy.
Wear goggles when you are welding.
Don't throw tools in the workshop.
Note *do not* would be used in a written notice or in a strong spoken instruction. Usually in speech we used the contracted form, *don't*.

... always check that all the safety guards are fitted correctly ... if you don't, someone might have a bad accident.

Note the use of *if* to talk about possible consequences if safety procedures aren't followed:
Always wear goggles when welding. If you don't, you might damage your eyes.
Never smoke in the workshop. If you do, you might start a fire.

British/American differences

British	American

Mind out!
This expression is only used in British English.

In both American and British English the expression *Watch out* is used. For example:

Mind you don't trip.	*Watch you don't trip.*
Mind your head!	*Watch your head!*

Dialogues 2

Flammable materials

A: Is that a no-smoking sign?

B: Yes, it is. As you know, some of the materials we use are highly-flammable so we have a very strict non-smoking policy in the factory.

A: What does that sign mean?

B: It means there must be no naked flames or sparks anywhere near flammable materials. If the materials ignite, it could cause a serious fire and the fumes they give off can be very dangerous if you inhale them.

The evacuation procedure

A: Could you just run through the evacuation procedure?

B: Yes, of course. When you hear the fire alarm, which is a very loud, continuous ringing noise, you should go to the nearest fire exit or fire escape as quickly as possible.

A: Should we use the stairs?

B: Yes, don't use the lifts. We have regular fire drills so you'll soon become familiar with the procedure. And always shut the fire doors to prevent the fire spreading.

Dealing with a fire

A: What should I do if I notice a fire?

B: Raise the alarm by breaking the glass of the nearest fire alarm. Call Security, say 'Fire' and give your name and exact location. At night you should phone the fire service from the nearest telephone.

A: Should I try to put the fire out?

B: If you discover a small fire, you can try to put it out with a fire extinguisher but only do this if you have been trained. Make sure you use the right extinguisher. They are all colour-coded and contain different substances to put out the fire.

Accident 1: A cut hand

A: Your hand is bleeding. What have you done to it?

B: I cut it on that blade.

A: I'll get the first aid box. There's some antiseptic cream and a bandage in there.

Accident 2: An ankle injury

A: Ow! I've twisted my ankle. I slipped on that greasy patch over there. I don't think it's broken but it really hurts.

B: Sit down here – don't put any pressure on it. I'd better call the company doctor.

Accident 3: A fall

A: Marco has fallen off a ladder. I think he's hurt his back. What shall we do?

B: We'd better not move him. I'll get the first-aider.

Notes

... some of the materials we use are highly-flammable ...

Instead of *are flammable* you could say: *catch fire/ignite/burn easily.*
Some of the materials we use burn easily.
Sometimes the word *inflammable* is used (e.g. *highly inflammable aircraft fuel*) with the same meaning as *flammable.*

... the fumes they give off can be very dangerous ...

Produce/emit can be used for *give off.*

Could you just run through the evacuation procedure?

You could use *go through* or *explain* for *run through:*
Could you explain/go through the safety instructions again?
To *evacuate* means to move people from a dangerous place.

When you hear the fire alarm, ... go to the nearest fire exit or fire escape ...

Note these expressions with *fire.*
Also: *a fire drill, the fire service, fire fighters.*

... always shut the fire doors to prevent the fire spreading.

You can also use *stop* for *prevent:*
The best thing is to stop the fire starting in the first place.
Prevent can be used with just a noun:
We must try to prevent accidents.

Raise the alarm by breaking the glass ...

Raise the alarm means warn people of danger.

... you can try to put it out with a fire extinguisher ...

To *put out* and to *extinguish* mean the same.
Note the word order: *Try to put out the fire.*
or: *Try to put the fire out.*
Be careful with the word order with *it: Try to put it out* (Note: **NOT** *put out it*)

Your hand is bleeding.

Some other injuries:
I've twisted my ankle.
I've got something in my eye.

I'll get the first aid box.

Note we use *I'll* to show that the speaker is going to take immediate action. A *first aid box* contains items such as scissors, plasters etc. to treat minor injuries.

... it really hurts.

It hurts means something is painful:
My arm hurts.

I'd better call the company doctor.

Note the use of *I/you/we had better* to talk about the correct thing to do in a difficult situation.
Had is usually shortened to *'d*. We don't use *to* after *had better* (Note: **NOT** *I'd better to call ...*)

I think he's hurt his back.

We can also say:
I think he's injured his back.

What shall we do?

Note the use of *shall I/we* to ask for an opinion on the correct thing to do.
Shall I call an ambulance?

We'd better not move him.

Note the negative form.

I'll get the first-aider.

A *first-aider* is someone in the workplace who has been given basic medical training to help people who have an accident or are ill at work.

British/American differences	
British	**American**
non-smoking policy	no smoking policy
lifts	elevators
To raise the alarm.	To sound the alarm
the fire service (also known as the fire brigade)	the fire department
the first-aider	

There is no *first-aider* equivalent in American English. You would see *the company doctor* or *nurse* in an American company, but this would be a professionally trained person.

plasters	Band-Aids (Band-Aid is a trademark)

Practice

1 Match the hazard with the possible result.

1	a live wire	a	you might be hit
2	a loose piece of flooring	b	you might slip over
3	a sharp blade	c	you might damage your hearing
4	steam	d	you might burn yourself
5	a careless truck driver	e	you might electrocute yourself
6	a greasy floor	f	you might cut yourself
7	a very loud noise	g	you might trip over

2 Complete the sentences with words from the box below.

when	you	mind	oil	out	tools	don't	careful	hot	sharp	floor	low

a   Mind . . . . don't trip. There are lots of . . . . lying around.

b   Be . . . . ! Don't touch the blades. They're very . . . .

c   Mind . . . . ! Someone's left some boxes on the . . . .

d   . . . . your heads! The doorway is very . . . .

e   Be careful . . . . you walk across the factory. There are often patches of

. . . . on the floor.

f   Mind you . . . . burn yourself. The metal is very . . . .

3 Match the two parts of the sentences.

1	Always wear ear protection	a	check electrical installations regularly.
2	Don't leave	b	emergency exits clear.
3	Keep	c	a machine without checking the safety procedures first.
4	Never place	d	when using a pneumatic drill.
5	Make sure you	e	bottles of chemicals carefully.
6	Check that	f	a ladder near an electricity line.
7	Do not operate	g	tools lying on the floor.
8	Label	h	the safety guard is in place.

4 Choose *It* or *There*.

EXAMPLE: . . It . .might be slippery.

a   . . . . might be very noisy.

b   . . . . might be a lot of dust.

c   . . . . might be very sharp.

d   . . . . might be trucks unloading.

e   . . . . might be bits of broken glass on the floor.

f   . . . . might be live.

5 What might happen if you don't follow safety procedures? First match the sentences.

1	Never store cylinders by naked flames.	a	Someone might slip over.
2	Always wear gloves when welding.	b	Someone may get poisoned.
3	You must wipe spillages up immediately.	c	They may explode.
4	You mustn't store chemicals in milk bottles or jam jars.	d	Someone might trip over them.
5	Never leave bits of wood lying around on the floor.	e	You might burn your hands.

Now choose *If you do,* or *If you don't,* to join the two sentences. Write out the whole sentences below.

EXAMPLE: Never store cylinders near naked flames. If you do,
................they may explode.

a ....

....

b ....

....

c ....

....

d ....

....

6 Rearrange these words to form questions.

a it/where/hurt/does? ....

b move/arm/you/can/your? ....

c happen/it/did/how? ....

d get/the/I/shall/first-aider? ....

e keep/first aid/where/we/box/do/the? ....

f injured/anyone/been/has? ....

g anyone/ambulance/has/yet/called/an? ....

h your/to/what/done/have/you/hand? ....

7 Match the sentences on the left with the responses on the right.

1 I think I've twisted my ankle.
2 I've cut my finger.
3 Look! The warehouse is on fire.
4 José has fallen and hurt his back.
5 I've splashed some chemical on my skin.
6 Maria has inhaled some fumes.
7 The machine is making a funny noise.
8 We haven't got any bandages.

a We'd better order some more.
b We'd better take her out into the fresh air.
c We'd better not use it. Switch it off!
d You'd better not put any pressure on it.
e You'd better put a plaster on it.
f You'd better wash it off immediately.
g We'd better not move him.
h We'd better call the fire service.

8 Fire vocabulary crossword.

Across

1 Move people from a dangerous place. (8) (v)
4 Catches fire easily. (9) (adj)
6 A door for leaving a building when there is a fire. (4,4) (n)
9 A metal cylinder containing water or chemical at high pressure used for putting out fires. (4,12) (n)
10 Burning gases in pointed shapes that come from something on fire. (6) (n)
11 To be on fire. (4) (v)

Down

2 Something like a bell that makes a loud noise to warn people of danger. (5) (n)
3 A small piece of bright burning material that flies up from something burning. (5) (n)
4 These practice what to do if there is a fire. (4,6) (n)
5 To catch fire or set fire to. (6) (v)
6 Unhealthy smoke, gas or smells produced when something burns. (5)
7 To extinguish. (3,3) (v)
8 The fire . . . . is the organisation which has the job of putting out fires. (7) (n)

9 Environmental matters

Some useful phrases.
Listen to the recording and repeat.

Plastics aren't bio-degradable.
They don't break down easily in the environment.
In what ways are your products environmentally-friendly?
We use recycled fibre in our boxes.

We've managed to reduce our energy consumption by 15 per cent.
We don't use any fossil fuels.
We use energy from alternative sources.

How do you dispose of the waste in your factory?
We have to send it to landfill.
We're planning to build a new incineration plant next year.
It's less harmful to the environment.

What damage does ozone do?
It's one of the main air pollutants.
Factories don't emit it directly into the air.

Has your company been affected much by government legislation?
We've had to meet tough government standards.
Are factories allowed to discharge waste water into the lake?
What happens if you exceed the limits?

Dialogues 1

Recycling

A: Recycling is big business these days, isn't it?

B: Yes, it's definitely a growing business.

A: What do you recycle in your plant?

B: Mainly plastics. Plastics aren't bio-degradable – they don't break down easily in the environment – so they shouldn't be thrown away.

A: How is plastic recycled, then?

B: Well, there are basically two methods. One is to break down the chemicals in the plastic into smaller chemical particles. These can then be used in the production of new chemicals.

A: Is that the method you use here?

B: No, we don't do that here. We recycle polyethylene and we make it into other products.

A: How do you do that?

B: By melting it down and then reforming it. Our main products are bin liners for kitchen bins and carrier bags for supermarkets.

Environmentally-friendly products

A: You say your products are aimed at the green consumer. In what ways are they environmentally-friendly?

B: We produce household cleaning products – detergents and so on. They are all phosphate-free, which minimises damage to the environment.

A: What about the packaging?

B: We try to use as little packaging as possible. Also, all our bottles are made of recyclable plastic and we use recycled fibre in our boxes. That's what our customers want.

Energy

A: We've managed to reduce our energy consumption in our factory by about 15 per cent in the last two years.

B: That's excellent. How have you managed that?

A: Mainly because we've invested in a heat recovery system.

A: What does that mean exactly?

B: Well, we use the exhaust gases from our printing presses to provide energy to heat our dryers.

A: What other sources of energy do you use?

B: We don't use any fossil fuels. Most of our power comes from hydro-electric plants. We're hoping to use even more energy from alternative sources in the future – perhaps even wind power.

Notes

Plastics aren't bio-degradable ...

Note the use of -*able*, which means that something is possible.
All our bottles are recyclable.
Wood is a renewable resource.
We produce disposable cigarette lighters.

... they don't break down easily in the environment ...

When a substance *breaks down*, it changes into a different form because of a chemical or biological process.
... in the environment here means *outside* (after being thrown away). Note the use of *the*.

... we make it into other products.

Note the use of *into* to indicate change.
Wind power can be converted into energy.

By melting it down ...

Note the use of *by* + verb+*ing* to talk about how something is done:
We've reduced our energy bill by investing in good insulation.

In what ways are they environmentally-friendly?

Environmentally-friendly means not so damaging to the environment:
It's environmentally unacceptable to dump waste in rivers.
Before a noun we use *environmental*:
Our environmental policy needs to be reviewed.
Pollution is causing big environmental changes.

They are all phosphate-free, ...

This means they don't contain *phosphates* (chemical compounds which are harmful to the environment). Other examples with -*free*:
Our paper is totally chlorine-free.
The engine runs on lead-free petrol.

... we use recycled fibre in our boxes.

This means that the board used for the boxes contains pulp made from paper or cardboard products.

We've managed to reduce our energy consumption ...

energy consumption is the amount of energy used. Note the verb *consume*:
We consume far too much fuel.

... by about 15 per cent ...

by is used to indicate the amount of increase or decrease in something.

... we've invested in a heat recovery system.

To *recover* means to *get back*. *Heat recovery* is a way of re-using heat or steam generated in the production process. Also note the use of *in* after *invest*.

We don't use any fossil fuels.

A *fossil fuel* is a fuel such as coal, oil or peat. When these fuels are burnt, they give off *greenhouse gases*, which contribute to *global warming*.

... energy from alternative sources ...

This refers to energy from more natural sources, e.g. wind power, solar energy (from the sun), hydro-electric power (from fast running water).

British/American differences	
British	**American**
bin liners	trash can liners
carrier bags	paper bags/plastic bags (also used in British English)
the green consumer	the environmentally aware/concerned customer (also used in British English).
minimises	minimizes
recycled fibre	recycled fiber
gases	gases/gasses

Dialogues 2

Disposing of waste

A: How do you dispose of the waste in your factory?

B: We try to recycle as much as we can.

A: What about the rest? How do you get rid of it?

B: We have to send it to landfill. It's very expensive because the government recently introduced a landfill tax so we're planning to build a new incineration plant next year to burn our waste.

A: But doesn't incineration produce carbon monoxide?

B: Yes, you're right, it does. But we believe it's less harmful to the environment than landfill.

Air pollution

A: I've heard of ground-level ozone but can you explain what it is exactly?

B: Yes, it's one of the main air pollutants. Factories don't emit it directly into the air. It's actually formed when nitrogen oxides and VOC emissions come into contact with heat and sunlight.

A: Sorry? What does VOC stand for?

B: Oh, VOCs are 'volatile organic compounds'. That's a technical term for solvents or other chemicals found in things like paint.

A: So, what damage does ozone do to the environment?

B: Well, it can cause smog, which can affect people's health – especially people with breathing difficulties.

Water pollution

A: Is the lake very polluted?

B: Well, I wouldn't swim in it – but the water is much cleaner than it was a few years ago.

A: Are local factories allowed to discharge waste water into the lake?

B: Yes, but it must be treated in an effluent treatment plant first.

Legislation

A: Has your company been affected much by government legislation?

B: Yes, we have. We've had to clean up our production process a lot to meet tough government standards.

A: What about your use of raw materials?

B: Well, we've had to cut down the amount of solvents we use and we're not allowed to use lead in our products any more.

A: What happens if you exceed the limits?

B: We try not to because you might have to pay quite a heavy fine.

Notes

How do you dispose of the waste in your factory?

You could also say:
How do you get rid of your waste?
Note also *disposal:*
Safe disposal of waste is important.

We have to send it to landfill.

A *landfill site* is a hole in the ground for rubbish.

... we're planning to build a new incineration plant next year ...

An *incineration plant* is where rubbish is burnt.

... it's less harmful to the environment than landfill.

It doesn't damage the environment as much as landfill.
It's better for the environment than landfill.

... can you explain what it is exactly?

Note the word order.
Note: **NOT** *Can you explain what is it?*

... it's one of the main air pollutants.

Other major industrial air pollutants are sulphur dioxide (SO_2), nitrogen dioxide (NO_2) and carbon dioxide (CO_2).

Factories don't emit it directly into the air.

To *emit* means to release gases into the air.
Note also *emissions:*
We need to reduce CO_2 emissions.

... what damage does ozone do to the environment?

You could use *harm* for *damage:*
What harm does ozone do?

... it can cause smog, which can affect people's health ...

Smog is a mixture of fog and smoke, found in polluted industrial areas. Note there is no preposition after *affect* (vb). The noun is spelt: *effect.*

Are local factories allowed to discharge waste water into the lake?

Be allowed to is used here for permission:
We're allowed to send some of our waste to landfill.
We're not allowed to use lead in our products.

... it must be treated in an effluent treatment plant first.

An *effluent treatment plant* is where liquid waste material (*effluent*) is cleaned up before being released.

Has your company been affected much by government legislation?

Legislation means *laws:*
New packaging legislation will be brought in next year.

... to meet tough government standards.

Tough here means *difficult.* You could also say *strict. Meet* here means to *satisfy:*
That product doesn't meet our requirements.

... we've had to cut down the amount of solvents we use ...

Cut down here means the same as *reduce.*
Note the use of *we've had to* to show that something is obligatory.

What happens if you exceed the limits?

Exceed the limits means to break the law or the rules by going over the permitted level.

British/American differences	
British	**American**
incineration plant	incinerating plant
office-paper recycling scheme, p77	office-paper recycling program (in American English *scheme* has the connotations of doing something bad or illegal).
send it to landfill	send it to a landfill

Practice

1 Complete the sentences with _are allowed to/aren't allowed to_ or _have to_.

EXAMPLE: We ..have to..... reduce our CO_2 emissions by 5 per cent by next year.

a Factories .... dump rubbish in the river. They can be fined if they do.

b Manufacturers .... follow strict environmental guidelines.

c The Governments sets strict limits on landfill. We .... send only 50 per cent of our waste to landfill sites. We .... recycle the rest.

d Paint producers .... use lead in their paint any more because it's a health hazard.

e We .... exceed the permitted levels.

2 Match the two parts of the sentences.

1 You can be fined   a by using a heat recovery process.

2 Our products minimise damage   b for breaking pollution laws.

3 Most plastics don't bio-degrade   c to the environment.

4 We're hoping to use more energy   d in the environment.

5 We can save energy   e from alternative sources.

3 Complete each sentence with a preposition or leave blank if no preposition is needed.

a We must get rid .... our waste in an acceptable way.

b The new legislation will affect .... everyone in the packaging industry.

c Is it harmful .... the environment?

d Safe disposal .... toxic substances is very important.

e Ozone is not emitted .... the atmosphere.

f Radiation from the sun can be converted .... electricity.

g Incineration is better .... the environment than landfill.

h Our budget for environmental projects will have to increase .... 10 per cent.

4 Complete the sentences with the correct verb.

EXAMPLE: When fossil fuels are burnt, they ..give.......... off CO_2. _give/take/send_

a We need to .... up our production process. _clear/take/clean_

b We are trying to .... down the amount of packaging we use. _put/cut/bring_

c You can .... down plastic and make it into a different product. _heat/cut/melt_

d It's better to recycle glass bottles than to .... them away. _throw/put/take_

e Most hamburger boxes don't .... down in the environment. _take/bring/break_

f The EU will .... in new legislation next year. _bring/put/call_

5 Complete the sentences with a word from the box below.

recycling	pollution	environmentally	disposable
environmental	dispose	~~recyclable~~	pollutants

EXAMPLE: Most types of paper are .recyclable...

a   There are six main air . . . .

b   We are setting up an . . . . management system.

c   We need to find a better way to . . . . of our waste.

d   It's an . . . . friendly product.

e   We have an office-paper . . . . scheme in our company.

f   . . . . is having an effect on the world climate.

g   They manufacture cheap . . . . cigarette lighters.

6 Rearrange these words to form questions.

EXAMPLE: plastic / how / be / can / recycled?
        .How can plastic be recycled?. . . . .

a   you / limits / happens / if / permitted / the / what / exceed?
     . . . .

b   of / you / waste / how / products / your / dispose / do?
     . . . .

c   VOCs / explain / are / can / you / what?
     . . . .

d   affected / recent / your / been / by / company / much / legislation / has?
     . . . .

e   you / of / what / sources / use / other / energy / do?
     . . . .

f   ways / environmentally / products / are / in / your / what / friendly?
     . . . .

g   does / ozone / environment / what / do / the / damage / to?
     . . . .

h   heat / explain / is / recovery / what / could / you?
     . . . .

7 Environmental vocabulary crossword

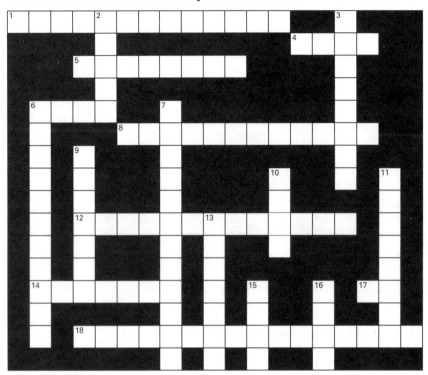

Across

1 CO$_2$. (6,7) (n)

4 A mixture of smoke and ozone. (4) (n)
5 They are found in paint and are bad for the environment. (8) (n)
6 What you may have to pay if you break a law. (4) (n)
8 A place where waste is put into a hole in the ground. (8,4) (n)
12 Able to break down naturally in the environment. (3,10) (adj)
14 Gases released into the atmosphere from a running engine. (7) (n)
17 Abbreviation for polyethylene. (2) (n)
18 Energy generated from fast running water. (5,11) (n)

Down

2 A gas which can cause problem for people with breathing difficulties. (5) (n)
3 Made dirty with chemicals, rubbish, etc. (8) (adj)
6 Coal, oil, etc. When burnt, they give off 1 across. (6,5) (n)
7 A method of disposing of waste by burning it. (12) (n)
9 Another word for waste. (7) (n)
10 In many countries petrol does not contain this any more. (4) (n)
11 Waste water. (8) (n)
13 To use again in a different process. (7) (v)
15 A technical term for 5 across. (4) (n)
16 To release into the atmosphere. (4) (v)

Word list

U refers to the Unit in the book. For example, U3 = Unit 3.

adhesive (n)
U3 — a substance used for sticking surfaces together

adjust (v)
U6, U7 — to make a correction by making a small change (e.g. to a machine setting)

aligned (adj)
U6 — brought into the correct position (in relation to another object)

apprentice (n)
U1 — a young person who is training to learn a skill for a job

assemble (v)
U1 — to put together

attachment (n)
U7 — (IT) a file sent with an email

axle (n)
U3 — a rod connecting a pair of wheels

backup (n)
U6, U7 — (IT) an extra copy of a computer file

bandage (n)
U8 — a long piece of white cloth which you wrap around an injured part of the body

bearings
U3, U7 — part of a machine which supports or holds another part which turns or moves

blade (n)
U2, U7, U8 — a flat piece of metal with a sharp edge used for cutting

bottleneck (n)
U2 — a blockage which prevents progress in production

break down (v)
U4, U6 — to stop working (a machine)

cabling (n)
U5 — large bundles of wires which carry electricity

calibrate (v)
U6 — to adjust something so that it measures accurately

canvas (n)
U6 — strong heavy cloth (often made of cotton)

carry out (v)
U5, U6 — to do (e.g. a repair, a test)

casing (n)
U6 — a protective cover (e.g. of a machine or machine part)

catering (n)
U4 — the supplying of food and drink on a large scale

civil engineer (n)
U5 — a person who designs things like roads, bridges, public buildings, etc.

coat (v)
U2 — to cover with a thin layer of something

component (n)
U1, U6 — a part

condemn (v)
U5 — to decide officially that a building is not safe for use

construction (n)
U1, U5 — the building of buildings, roads, bridges, etc.

container (n)
U5 — a large metal box used for transporting goods

conveyor belt (n)
U2, U6 — a series of metal rollers or a belt which move objects around a factory

corroded (adj)
U6 — eaten away by a chemical such as strong acid or rust

corrosion (n)
U6 — the damage caused when something has corroded (e.g. rust)

courier (n)
U4 — a person who delivers an important document or parcel

crash (v)
U7 — (IT) to suddenly fail/break down

crate (n)
U3 — a large box used for carrying or storing things (usually made of wood)

crew (n)
U5 — a team of workers

cursor (n)
U7 — (IT) a flashing symbol which shows the position on a computer screen

cut out (v)
U7 — to suddenly stop working (e.g. a motor)

database (n)
U7 — (IT) information and facts stored in a computer

delay (n)
U5 — an unexpected wait that causes something to happen late

detergent (n)
U9 — a chemical powder or liquid used for cleaning things

diagnostic (adj)
U6 — used for discovering what is wrong with something that is not working properly

diameter (n)
U3 — the length of a straight line drawn through the centre of something round

discharge (v) U9	to release a substance into water or the air	**foundry** (n) U2	a place where metal is melted and made into new objects
dispatch (v) U4	to send	**fumes** (n) U8	the unpleasant, unhealthy smoke produced by fires or chemicals
diversify (v) U1	to start producing new and different products	**fuse** (n) U7	a electrical safety device consisting of a thin piece of wire which melts to stop the flow of electricity
domestic (adj) U1	the home country		
dump (v) U9	to throw away (e.g. rubbish)	**fuse- box** (n) U7	a box containing the fuses for all the electrical circuits in a certain area
electrocute yourself (v) U8	to be killed or badly injured after touching something which is directly connected to a source of electricity	**gasket** (n) U6	a flat piece of material put between two joined surfaces in a pipe or engine to prevent gas, oil, etc. escaping
exhaust gases/ fumes (n) U9	gases produced by running engines	**gatehouse** (n) U2	a small building at the entrance to a factory site
expand (v) U7	to become larger in size or amount	**gauge** (n) U6	an instrument that measures something
extract (v) U2	to take something out of something	**gears** (n) U7	a device (often consisting of wheels with teeth) for connecting the moving parts of a machine and which controls the speed and direction of movement
feeder (n) U2	a machine or device which supplies something (e.g. a part) to another machine		
filter (n) U2	a piece of equipment that you pass liquid or gas through to remove particles	**generator** (n) U1	a machine that produces electricity
fine (n) U9	money paid as a punishment	**global warming** (n) U9	the warming of the earth's atmosphere
fire alarm (n) U8	a loud bell or buzzer that warns of a fire	**greenhouse gases** (n) U9	gases which cause the earth's temperature to rise
fire drill (n) U8	a practice of the evacuation procedure in a fire	**grinding** (n) U3	making something smooth or sharp using friction
fire escape (n) U8	a metal staircase on the outside of a building or a route which can be used to leave a building safely in case of emergency	**guarantee** (n) (and v) U4	a written promise by a company to repair faults on something they have supplied for a specified length of time
flash (v) U7	if a light flashes, it goes on and off repeatedly	**hose** (n) U3	a flexible pipe
foreman (n) U1	a person who is responsible for a group of workers	**icon** (n) U7	(IT) a symbol on a computer screen that represents a program or a file
fork-lift truck (n) U8	a vehicle with two moveable arms at the front which are placed under heavy objects to lift them and transport them	**inhale** (v) U8	to breathe in (take in air)

insulation (n) U9	a thick, warm layer of a material which keeps in heat	**preventive** (adj) U6	designed to stop something bad happening
inventory (n) U3	a list of all the items in a particular place	**print head** (n) U6	(IT) the part of a printer which holds the ink
invoice (n) U4	a document listing goods or services supplied and the money owed	**properly** (adv) U6	in the correct way
laptop (n) U4	(IT) a small personal computer that can be carried around	**pulp** (n) U2	a very thick liquid made from crushed wood used to make paper
lead (n) U9	Pb (chemical symbol)	**pump** (n) U2, U6	a machine which is used to force a liquid or gas to flow in a particular direction
leak (n) U7	an escape of liquid or gas, e.g. from a pipe	**recruiting** (n) U4	finding new employees
light bulb (n) U3	the round glass part of a light through which the light shines	**reel** (n) U2	a cylinder around which things are wound
live wire (n) U8	a wire directly connected to a source of electricity	**refinery** (n) U2	a place where oil is processed
lubricant (n) U3	a substance such as oil applied to parts of a machine to reduce friction	**replace** (v) U4, U6	to put in something new to do the same job
lubricate (v) U6	to apply a lubricant	**replacement** (n) U4, U6, U7	something or someone that takes the place of another thing or person
monitor (v) U2	to make regular checks on progress	**reservoir** (n) U3	a natural or artificial lake used for storing water
naked flame (n) U8	an uncovered flame	**restore** (v) U7	(IT) get back again (e.g. a file or data)
offline (adj) U5	(IT) not connected to the Internet or a network	**robot** (n) U2	a machine which is programmed to perform mechanical tasks
on site (adj) U4, U5, U6	at the place (e.g. a factory) where a business is carried out	**rollers** (n) U2, U6	rotating cylinders in a machine
oversee (v) U5	to make sure that something (e.g. a project) is done correctly	**rot** (v) U6	to decay and break into pieces and become unusable
pallet (n) U2, U8	a wooden platform that goods are packed on	**routine** (adj) U6	done on a regular basis as part of the normal procedure
particle (n) U9	a very small piece	**safety guard** (n) U8	a device which covers a dangerous part of a machine
perish (v) U6	if something such as rubber perishes, it starts to decay and break into pieces	**sawing** (n) U3	cutting something with a saw (a tool with a blade with sharp teeth)
plaster (n) U8	a small piece of sticky fabric used for covering small cuts on the body	**schedule** (n) (and v) U5	a plan with a list of things to be done and the times they should be done
pollutant (n) U9	a substance (e.g. a poisonous gas) which pollutes the environment		

seal (n) U6, U7	something that closes an opening tightly to stop air, gas or liquid getting in or out
sensor (n) U6	an instrument which notices physical changes and gives information to a monitor
server (n) U7	(IT) a computer used for storing and managing programs and data used by other computers
shift (n) U1	a period of time (e.g. eight hours) when a group of people are working (can also mean the group of workers who work on a shift)
shop (n) U1	an area in a factory where things are made or done (e.g. the assembly shop, the repair shop)
shut, shutdown (n) (and v) U6	the period when a machine is not producing due to a breakdown or for maintenance
slippery (adj) U8	difficult to walk on because the surface is wet, greasy, icy, etc. so you might fall
snap off (v) U7	to suddenly break off and become separate
software (n) U5	(IT) the programs that make a computer operate
solvent (n) U2, U9	a liquid that can dissolve other substances
spark (n) U8	a very small piece of burning material that flies up from a burning object
spillage (n) U8	liquid that has spilt (i.e. fallen from a container)
splash (v) U8	if liquid splashes you, it hits you in small drops
stationery (n) U7	items such as paper, pens and envelopes needed in an office
supervisor (n) U1, U7, U8	a person who is responsible for a group of workers
stock check (n) U3	the counting of all the goods in a shop, warehouse or stores to keep records up to date

toner cartridge (n) U7	a container of ink for photocopier or printer
top up (v) U7	to fill something up again that has been partly emptied
toxic (adj) U8, U9	poisonous
tray (n) U2, U6	a flat piece of metal, plastic, etc. with raised edges used for holding something (e.g. liquid or paper)
trip (over something) (v) U8	to knock your foot against something when you are walking so that you fall or nearly fall
twist your ankle (v) U8	to injure the joint between your foot and your leg by turning it sharply
unplug something (v) U8	to take the plug out of an electric socket
upgrade (n) U5 (v) U7	an improvement of a machine or system by adding to it to allow it to do more or perform better
urgent (adj) U6	needing immediate attention
valve (n) U4, U7	a device in a tube which controls the flow of liquid, air, electricity etc. by opening and closing
version (n) U7	(IT) something (e.g. a program) that differs in detail from an earlier or later form of it
warranty (n) U4	similar to a guarantee
wear out/down (v) **worn out/down** (adj) U6	to gradually become in poor condition and therefore unusable
welding (n) U3	joining metal together using heat
workstation (n) U2	the area where part of the assembly of a product is carried out (e.g. in a car factory)

Glossary

1 Telephoning

Dialogues 1
	Your language
I work for a large multinational company.	....
We manufacture car components for our car production plants in Europe.	....
The company has operations in over fifty countries.	....
We specialise in medium-sized generators.	....
We export to Eastern Europe and the Far East.	....
The domestic market accounts for about 40 cent of our total sales.	....
We have over sixty employees.	....
We have about forty factory workers and technical people.	....
The rest are admin and sales staff.	....
Our workforce has grown a lot.	....
What's your annual turnover?	....
The original company was founded in 1960.	....
What does IABS stand for?	....

Dialogues 2
I'm an apprentice.	....
I hope the company will take me on as an engineer.	....
What does your job involve?	....
I have to make sure our projects run smoothly.	....
I'm in charge of about twenty-five assembly workers.	....
I have to liaise very closely with our inspectors.	....
Who do you report to?	....
Each team member is responsible for the quality of the goods we produce.	....
We are multi-skilled so we can rotate jobs.	....
I'm on flexi-time.	....
I usually take two weeks off in the summer.	....
Do you do overtime?	....
I'm paid double-time if I work at weekends.	....
We have a three-shift system.	....
I'm on the early shift.	....

2 A tour of the workplace

Dialogues 1

	Your language
Park in the visitors' car park in front of the factory.	....
We used to be on an industrial estate on the outskirts of York.	....
We needed larger premises.	....
We moved to this greenfield site last year.	....
I'd like to show you the layout of the factory.	....
The main production area – our machine hall – is situated next to it.	....
This is the main factory area.	....
What's going on over there?	....
They're setting up the machine for a new run.	....
How long does that usually take?	....
The goods are being wrapped and loaded onto pallets.	....

Dialogues 2

Would you like me to show you our new cleaning unit?	....
What does the unit consist of?	....
This is our newest machine.	....
What's the running speed of the machine?	....
If we're running at full capacity, it's 160 000 tonnes per annum.	....
The pulp falls from a box onto the first part of the paper machine.	....
Most of the water is extracted.	....
It then passes through a series of rollers.	....
Is the factory fully-automated?	....
Some of the work is still done manually.	....
It's a bar-code system.	....

3 Tools and equipment

Dialogues 1

We've got very good workshop facilities.	....
We do all our own servicing.	....

84

Your language

Is there anything you don't do in-house? ....

We send it out for maintenance ....

It's actually more cost effective. ....

I need something to tighten it up. ....

No problem. ....

Where can I find a spare hose? ....

They're at the back of the stores, second shelf ....
   up on the right-hand side. ....

We don't have any in stock. ....

How many do you need? ....

The day after tomorrow. ....

What's it used for? ....

It's a really useful piece of equipment. ....

Dialogues 2

Don't forget to update the inventory! ....

Can you help me? ....

I need to measure the length of this workbench. ....

We're going to replace it. ....

Let's round it up to 3.50. ....

Could we increase it by about a third? ....

We need a piece of wood 3.5 m long by 1 m wide. ....

Install it next Tuesday. ....

Can you shorten this pipe? ....

Can you take 15 mm off it? ....

What does it look like? ....

It's oblong-shaped. ....

It's made of metal. ....

4 Suppliers and sub-contractors

Dialogues 1

We look for companies with a good track record. ....

We work to very low tolerance levels. ....

We've built up very good relationships with ....
   our suppliers. ....

There are about fifty names on our approved ....
   supplier list. ....

We tend to deal with three local companies. ....

Your language

At peak times we hire in casual workers. ....

We contract out certain services. ....

They always arrive within a couple of hours. ....

There's no call-out fee. It's all included in the ....
annual service contract. ....

Our usual supplier has let us down. ....

How soon can you deliver? ....

I can deliver those by first thing tomorrow morning. ....

There'll be an extra charge for special delivery. ....

I'll have to send them by courier. ....

Dialogues 2

I'm not happy with their response time. ....

I'd like to check the terms and conditions. ....

It's due for renewal at the end of next month. ....

Is it still under guarantee? ....

The guarantee's just run out. ....

We took out an extended warranty. ....

It runs until next March. ....

We offer a replacement unit free of charge. ....

We recommend you take out an extended ....
warranty. ....

What does that include? ....

Our engineers are on call 24 hours a day. ....

Are there any exclusions? ....

It's a very comprehensive warranty. ....

Read through the small print. ....

Our supplier has gone bust. ....

Our insurance policy covers us against ....
situations like this. ....

5 Buildings and installations

Dialogues 1

I'm a bit concerned about this. ....

What's the height clearance? ....

That's a good point. ....

When is the building work due to start? ....

It'll take three weeks to demolish the old
   building and clear away the debris.

How long will the sub-contractors be on site?

About ten weeks in total, if everything goes
   according to plan.

We've taken on a civil engineer on a
   nine-month temporary contract.

We need to allocate responsibilities.

We've had a slight delay.

We're working to a really tight schedule.

We're already over budget.

We can still meet the deadline.

The crew is on stand-by.

It must be ready on time.

Dialogues 2

The first phase of the project was finished
   three days ahead of schedule.

We're on target to complete phase two.

We're waiting for the safety inspector to give
   us the go-ahead to continue.

Is the new stock system in operation?

We trained on a dummy system.

This is the live system.

The program's going live on Monday.

The new programs will operate in tandem.

That should give us time to iron out any little
   problems.

How long will the system be down for?

We'll be taking everything offline in about
   two hours' time.

It'll be down for a minimum of twelve hours.

We've allowed forty-eight hours to be on the
   safe side.

6 Maintenance

Dialogues 1

	Your language
Someone has reported a fault.	....
When was it serviced?	....
It's usually very reliable.	....
It's probably just a minor fault.	....
I'll have a look at it.	....
Each head lasts about 5 000 copies or so.	....
This model's designed for heavy use.	....
They are complex machines.	....
We check this machine once a fortnight.	....
There is a canvas belt at the end of the assembly line.	....
I'd like to go over the list of jobs.	....
We're planning to shut the line at midday on Wednesday.	....
We might need to extend the shut by about six hours.	....
We've got a full order book.	....
Is there any way you could speed things up?	....

Dialogues 2

There have been too many unplanned shutdowns.	....
We need to reduce our downtime.	....
The maintenance team is fully stretched.	....
We need to establish routine maintenance procedures.	....
It's a crucial part of our process.	....
We clean it and flush it through.	....
We recalibrate the gauges weekly.	....
We can predict the lifespan of different components.	....
We try to replace components before they fail or wear out.	....
How often do you service the vans?	....
We give them a basic service every 10 000 km or so.	....
They get a lot of wear and tear.	....

We give the engines a major overhaul. . . . .

We strip down the engine and find the faulty . . . .

   component. . . . .

Once we have disconnected the unit we do as . . . .

   many jobs as we can. . . . .

We make a note in the service record. . . . .

7 Troubleshooting

Dialogues 1

Johan hasn't turned up. . . . .

Do we have anyone on stand-by? . . . .

We're very short-staffed at the moment. . . . .

Tommi can stand in for an hour. . . . .

Have you checked the fuse box? . . . .

The fuse had blown. . . . .

Check the settings on the trip-switch. . . . .

What's wrong with the photocopier? . . . .

The toner has run out. . . . .

The gears have seized up. . . . .

You'll have to dismantle the unit. . . . .

I think the valve is faulty. . . . .

I couldn't regulate the pressure. . . . .

The seal burst. . . . .

Dialogues 2

Do you know how to get rid of it? . . . .

Why don't you call the Help Desk? . . . .

I might have the wrong version. . . . .

You'll have to upgrade. . . . .

My screen is frozen. . . . .

Have you tried pressing the Escape key? . . . .

You'll need to reboot your machine. . . . .

When did you last take a backup? . . . .

I've been having problems getting onto the . . . .

   Internet.

The server might be down. . . . .

The system keeps crashing. . . . .

8 Safety in the workplace

Dialogues 1

Your language

It's quite a hazardous environment. ....

You should put your ear plugs in. ....

You mustn't smoke here. ....

You must wear goggles in that area. ....

Mind out! Don't get too close. ....

Please be careful when you walk across the floor. ....

It might be slippery. ....

There might be a fork-lift truck reversing into
   the storage area. ....

Some of you are already familiar with the
   safety procedures. ....

Make sure you know how to stop the machine. ....

Always check that all the safety guards are
   fitted correctly. ....

If you don't, someone might have a bad accident. ....

Dialogue 2

Some of the materials we use are highly-
   flammable. ....

The fumes they give off can be very dangerous. ....

Could you run through the evacuation
   procedure? ....

When you hear the fire alarm, go to the nearest
   fire exit or fire escape. ....

Always shut the fire doors to prevent the
   fire spreading. ....

Raise the alarm by breaking the glass. ....

You can try to put it out with a fire extinguisher. ....

Your hand is bleeding. ....

I'll get the first aid box. ....

It really hurts. ....

I'd better call the company doctor. ....

I think he's hurt his back. ....

What shall we do? ....

We'd better not move him. ....

I'll get the first-aider. ....

9 Environmental matters

Dialogues 1

Your language

Plastics aren't bio-degradable. ....

They don't break down easily in the environment. ....

We make it into other products by melting it down. ....

In what ways are they environmentally-friendly? ....

They are all phosphate-free. ....

We use recycled fibre in our boxes. ....

We've managed to reduce our energy ....

consumption by about 15 per cent. ....

We've invested in a heat recovery system. ....

We don't use any fossil fuels. ....

We're hoping to use more energy from ....

alternative sources. ....

Dialogue 2

How do you dispose of the waste in your factory? ....

We have to send it to landfill. ....

We're planning to build a new incineration ....

plant next year. ....

It's less harmful to the environment than landfill. ....

Can you explain what it is exactly? ....

It's one of the main air pollutants. ....

Factories don't emit it directly into the air. ....

What damage does ozone do to the environment? ....

It can cause smog, which can affect people's ....

health. ....

Are factories allowed to discharge waste water ....

into the lake? ....

It must be treated in an effluent treatment plant ....

first. ....

Has your company been affected much by ....

government legislation? ....

We've had to meet tough government standards. ....

We've had to cut down the amount of solvents ....

we use. ....

What happens if you exceed the limits? ....

Answers

1 Working in industry

1
a Who do you work for?
b What does your company do exactly?
c How many people does your company employ?
d What do you do?
e What does your job involve?
f Who do you report to?
g How many hours do you work a week?
h What's your annual turnover?

2   a for   b for   c over   d in   e into   f for   g for   h of   i of   j with

3   a overtime   b apprentice   c flexi-time   d operations   e shift   f workforce
g components   h people   i plant

4   1 e   2 h   3 b   4 a   5 f   6 i   7 d   8 j   9 c   10 g

5   a take   b look   c close/shut   d take   e set/start

6   a the   b –   c –   d –   e the   f the   g –   h –   i –   j the

7   a lab technician   b machine operator   c fitter   d electrician   e welder   f mechanic
g inspector   h production planner   i electronic engineer

2 A tour of the workplace

1
a The smaller models are made in our French factory.
b The paper is printed on both sides.
c The A-line is being repaired at the moment.
d The plastic is then wound onto reels.
e The blades are changed twice a week.
f The finished goods are being loaded onto lorries.
g A new plant is being built just outside Cape Town.
h The components are selected automatically.

2   a at   b onto   c to   d of   e into   f to   g at   h At   i through   j to

3   a outskirts   b brownfield   c gatehouse   d conveyor   e premises   f bar-codes
g capacity   h layout   i estate

4

	Order
a The paper is dried with hot air.	7
b The pulp is dropped onto the paper machine.	5
c The pieces of wood are broken down into fibres.	3
d The fibres are mixed with water to make pulp.	4
e The wood is cut into little pieces.	2
f The reels are transported to the customers.	9
g The trees are cut down.	1
h Water is extracted from the paper.	6
i The paper is wound onto reels.	8

5   1 d   2 f   3 a   4 e   5 b   6 c

6 a oil refinery   b steel works/mill   c coal mine   d shipyard   e nuclear reactor
f chocolate factory   g cotton mill

7 a between   b next to/to the left of   c opposite   d behind   e opposite   f next to/to the right of

3 Tools and equipment

1 a at; of   b by   c by   d for   e of   f by   g in

2 a wide   b width   c long   d lengthen   e length   f deep   g depth   h high   i height

3 a round   b check   c loosen   d stored   e facilities   f workbench   g tape

4 **Across**
2 lathe   6 screwdriver   8 hammer   9 pliers   10 rag   11 nut   13 callipers   15 bolt   16 chisel
17 crate   18 sandpaper

Down
1 knife   3 hacksaw   4 drill   5 wire-cutters   6 spanner   7 workbench   10 ruler
12 nails   13 clamp   14 tongs

5 1 d   2 e   3 f   4 g   5 b   6 a   7 h   8 c

6 cylinder – cylindrical – cylindrical
sphere – spherical – sphere-shaped
pyramid – pyramid – pyramid
cube – cuboid – cube
oval – oval – oval
oblong – oblong – oblong; rectangle – rectangular – rectangle

4 Suppliers and subcontractors

1 a for   b of   c at   d within/in   e in   f out   g under   h up   i with

2 1 d   2 f   3 b   4 e   5 a   6 c

3 a suppliers   b comprehensive   c deal   d services   e tolerance   f reputation   g approved
h peak   i bust   j conditions   k charge

4 a in   b at   c until   d by   e during   f within   g at   h until   i within

5 wear and tear
parts and labour
goods and services
terms and conditions
repair and maintenance

6 a 've built up   b have gone bust   c runs out   d are   e 'll put   f hire in   g seems

7 a Is it/the product still under guarantee?/Is the guarantee still valid?
b Do you handle the recruiting yourselves?
c Do you have many suppliers?
d How soon can you deliver?
e When does the contract run out/is the contract due for renewal?
f What does the warranty/it include?; ... cover us for/against?
g How long is it valid?/How long does it last?

h Are there any exclusions?
i Do we have to pay extra (for that)?
j What does the warranty include?

5 Buildings and installation

1   a on   b on; in   c over   d behind   e for   f on

2   1 h   2 e   3 g   4 a   5 f   6 d   7 c   8 b

3   a for   b for   c in   d for   e in

4   a tandem   b go-ahead   c tight   d allowed   e demolish   f safety   g slight   h installed
       i live   j down   k testing

5   a arrive   b to complete   c goes   d is   e meet   f allowed   g finished   h is

6   a How are things going?
       b Is the system ready?/Is the new computerised system ready?
       c How long will the computer/network/system be down for?
       d What stage are you at?
       e What is the height clearance?

7   1 demolish   e
       2 sub-contractors   i
       3 permanent   a
       4 deadline   c
       5 software engineer   h
       6 go-ahead   b
       7 in operation   f
       8 on standby   d

6 Maintenance

1   a do   b make   c make   d do   e make

2   every two weeks – fortnightly
       hardly ever – rarely
       once a year – annually
       every week – weekly
       on a daily basis – once a day

3   1 d   2 e   3 f   4 a   5 b   6 c

4   a for   b under   c with   d at   e at   f in; next   g of   h on

5   a strip down   b worn down   c go over/through   d flush through   e look around   f set up
       g slow down

6   a essential   b moving   c capacity   d often   e dismantle

7   a unexpected   b recalibrate   c unlocked   d reprint   e dislodged   f disconnect
       g unleaded   h reorder   i disengage

8   1 d   2 c   3 e   4 f   5 b   6 a

9 a clean/drain//check/service/dismantle
b check/clean/service/replace
c check/lubricate/clean/dismantle/replace/service
d check/clean/replace
e check/top up
f recalibrate/check/clean/replace/service

7 Troubleshooting

1 a onto b on c into d in; on e with f out

2 a top up b run out c turn up d clean it up e switch off f cut out g seize up
h call in

3 1 f 2 e 3 h 4 b 5 d 6 g 7 c 8 a

4 a expand b crashed c jammed d restore e tripped f snapped g cursor h leak
i loose j fault k lubricated

5 a drain b adjusting c switch off d upgrade e replacing f close g cutting out

6 a The toner has run out.
b You'll need to expand your memory.
c You'll need to reboot your machine./Have you tried pressing the Escape key?
d Have you checked the fuse box?
e No, why don't you call the Help Desk?
f You'll have to dismantle the unit and lubricate the bearings.

8 Safety in the workplace

1 1 e 2 g 3 f 4 d 5 a 6 b 7 c

2 a you; tools b careful; sharp c out; floor d mind; low e when; oil f don't; hot

3 1 d 2 g 3 b 4 f 5 a 6 h 7 c 8 e

4 a It b There c It d There e There f It

5 1 c 2 e 3 a 4 b 5 d

a Always wear gloves when welding. If you don't, you might burn your hands.
b You must wipe spillages up immediately. If you don't, someone might slip over.
c You mustn't store chemicals in milk bottles or jam jars. If you do, someone may
get poisoned.
d Never leave bits of wood lying around on the floor. If you do, someone might
trip over them.

6 a Where does it hurt?
b Can you move your arm?
c How did it happen?
d Shall I get the first-aider?
e Where do we keep the first aid box?
f Has anyone been injured?
g Has anyone called an ambulance yet?
h What have you done to your hand?

7   1 d   2 e   3 h   4 g   5 f   6 b   7 c   8 a

8   **Across**

1 evacuate   4 flammable   6 fire exit   9 fire extinguisher   10 flames   11 burn

Down

2 alarm   3 spark   4 fire drills   5 ignite   6 fumes   7 put out   8 service

9 Environmental matters

1   a aren't allowed to
   b have to
   c are allowed to; have to
   d aren't allowed to
   e aren't allowed to

2   1 b   2 c   3 d   4 e   5 a

3   a of   b –   c to   d of   e into   f into   g for   h by

4   a clean   b cut   c melt   d throw   e break   f bring

5   a pollutants   b environmental   c dispose   d environmentally   e recycling   f Pollution
   g disposable

6   a What happens if you exceed the permitted limits?
   b How do you dispose of your waste products?
   c Can you explain what VOCs are?
   d Has your company been affected much by recent legislation?
   e What other sources of energy do you use?
   f In what ways are your products environmentally-friendly?
   g What damage does ozone do to the environment?
   h Could you explain what heat recovery is?

7   **Across**

1 carbon dioxide   4 smog   5 solvents   6 fine   8 landfill site   12 bio-degradable
14 exhaust   17 PE   18 hydro-electricity

Down

2 ozone   3 polluted   6 fossil fuels   7 incineration   9 rubbish   10 lead   11 effluent
13 recycle   15 VOCs   16 emit